7AGE

i

n'nocent
7age

Lyf is simply about
X'PRESSION

kw≡isi

three reign dropz Publishing, Chicago

Second Printing
Copyright 1999 by kweisi r. l. dunlap jr.
three reign dropz Publishing Chicago, Illinois

Cover & Book design by S.T. Grafics
Cover concept by kweisi
Make-up artist: Prosperity
Cover Photo by Kahlil Williams
Photos by Kahlil Williams (except pages 16, 23, 32, 33, 62, 68, 69, 84, 89, 90, 92, 93, 98)
Edited by Derrick K. Baker

Printed in the United States of America

Library of Congress
Cataloging-in-Publication-Data

dunlap, jr. kweisi r.l.
    n'nocent 7age/ kweisi r.l. dunlap jr.
p.   cm.
ISBN 0-9666444-0-9

three reign dropz Publishing
P.O. Box 14869
Chicago, IL 60611

Booking information:
three reign dropz Publishing
312.720.RAGE

Dedication

this book is dedikated 2 my mother diane. i thank you with an infinite of reign dropz for your patience. 2 my brother JLF (Lemont) in tha spiritual world, i steel sea you in my dreamz. 2 jessica care moore and sista von for bein' and be-komin' what U ought 2 b so, i kan b what i ought 2 b. one Luv. 2 my phamily, klose phriendz, 2 U tha people of Chicago for Listening to me on WGCI and embracing me as me. one Luv. i am bein' and bekoming what i need 2 be so, you kan bekome what you need 2 be. Peace!

Kontentz on tha table

Kontentz on tha table

Preface

I first met kweisi r.l. dunlap jr. as a result of a shared friendship with Wayne Noble Crockrom. Prior to our formal meeting I had often heard kweisi in the evening on 107.5 WGCI-FM radio on the Bad Boyz show with "phood pha tha souL" where he gave words of encouragement and inspiration on weeknights. So I believe it is fate that our lives have converged at this point and time. kweisi, as I have come to know him, is a true representation of a "Spirit Warrior" whose weapon of choice is the "Spoken Word." During the course of his growth and development, I have been impressed by his commitment and dedication to his culture and life in general.

His ability to weave and fashion words has allowed him to become a spoken word artist who causes an implosion throughout one's Mind, Body and Soul, shaking the very foundation of our essence of beingness and becoming one with Spirit, thus challenging us to be Mo'Better.

He has succeeded in compiling a unique collection of his spoken words entitled "n'nocent 7age," which I feel is one for the ages, young and old alike; a book that was created and realized after the death of his younger brother James Lemar Ford (Lemont) on January 11, 1992, after which kweisi was filled with Rage and Anger, feeling Hurt and Pain. He took a bold and powerful step by descending back into himself to ultimately saving himself from self-destruction. kweisi began to Rescue, Reconstruct, Resurrect a new view and a new relationship with himself and with GOD. By building upon the old foundation of our African Ancestors through the process, concept and principal of Sankofa (return and fetch it) by realizing that "It is not taboo to return and fetch it when you forget. You can always undo your mistakes." As a result of his struggle to find peace within, we are presented with his spoken words, which are a powerful combination of information and inspiration that offers Hope and a renewed sense of pride for Africans and an educational opportunity for everyone. He challenges us to see if we can benefit from the consequences of miseducation and offers an alternative to correct the situation.

He creatively pays tribute to Brother Gil Scott-Heron in "The Revolution Will be Televised" to the fact that it's being televised as we speak, or rather read. It is my hope that you, as I have, will begin to see the power of the spoken words be it "n'nocent 7age" or your own voice, speak on it because words are powerful and when connected to the right source, they too can become life- sustaining.

Hide nothing from the masses of our
people.
Tell no lies.
Expose lies wherever they are told.
Mask no difficulties, mistakes, failures.
Claim no easy victories.
Amilcar Cabral

Kwesi Ronald E. Harris,
Director, Alcohol, Tobacco and other Drug Prevention Programs
The Bobby E. Wright Comprehensive Community Mental Health Center (Chicago)

From my steel quite BLAK Sea

how kan i say, "i

believe n GOD, whom i've

neva seen and rephuse

2 believe n myself who

i Sea everyday"…

thank YOU for your reign dropz
kweisi
May 1998

INTRODUCTION

It was early Sunday morning on January 12, 1992. I was a senior at Central State University in Wilberforce, Ohio, living in the Kappa Alpha Psi fraternity house when I got the call.

"Yo! Bra, telephone!"

"Who is it?"

"It's your sister."

"Yeah, what's up?"

"Junior, somebody kidnapped Lemont!"

"What? I'm on my way home."

I got dressed immediately, filled my car up with gas and I was on the road to Chicago. Wilberforce to Chicago is about a five-hour trip; I got there in three. I was praying and hoping that Lemont was okay, that they wanted ransom money. At one point I flipped on the radio and twice caught the beginning of "It's So Hard to Say Goodbye to Yesterday" by Boyz II Men. I started crying. I knew the kidnappers had killed Lemont.

That horrible truth was confirmed when I walked into the house and I was embraced by my mother and sister Tonya. A couple of days later, I went to see my brother at the morgue. That's something I'll never forget.

Lemont was killed because he stepped in to help a female friend. He saved her life. They were approached by a brother about six doors from our house. A sawed-off 12 gauge ended his life execution style. The two brothers responsible for his murder, Eric Taylor and Jonathan Judkins, kidnapped Lemont, taking him three miles from our home and forcing him to strip of all clothing, leaving his naked body in a vacant lot. Two weeks later, when they were caught, Jonathan had on Lemont's pants and gym shoes. My family was in and out of court at least once a month from February 1992 to October 7, 1994. The two were convicted of first-degree murder and sentenced to life in prison, plus 30 years for kidnapping and 15 years for armed robbery.

Lemont, 17, was an innocent (n'nocent) victim of a violent crime and his death has propelled me to express my rage (7age, release anxiety to gain excellence) in a positive-sense passion. Initially, I thought of seeking retribution, but one of my frat brothers, Joey Gray, who I respect dearly advised me not to seek revenge, but to be strong for my family and most of all for myself.

Trying to deal with Lemont's murder has been a catalyst in my search for the Heavenly Mother/Father in my life. I was mad as hell, angry and I kept asking GOD, "Why?" I was so distraught, I was seconds away from committing suicide in July 1992, October 1994 and May 1996. I really didn't let go of Lemont's death until June 25, 1997, when I had a dream that some of my friends and I buried him. However, I am supposed to Love GOD more than my brother or anyone else. So I no longer look at Lemont's death as a tragedy but as a gift, because life is death and death is life, which is rebirth. I now ask for understanding, direction and wisdom so I can become a better person for HER\HIM, myself, my family and the community. GOD has also given me the strength to forgive Eric and Jonathan. I wrote them twice in prison, in October and November 1995. I met Eric (he was convicted of shooting Lemont. see, "It's Time for Brother to Make Real Peace," May 6, 1996, Chicago Defender, page 12) on April 28, 1996, to let him know I understand their struggle being young BLAK males in Amerikkka, and that I have no hatred or anger toward them. I was writing them because I want to make peace.

I was born kweisi, however, I was named robert lee dunlap, jr. on Sunday, December 28, 1969, to

Diane Marie and Robert Lee Dunlap. I have two older sisters, Tracey M. and Rosetta L. Dunlap, and a younger brother James Lemar Ford (Lemont). I was disciplined on the South Side of Chicago on 123rd and Loomis. I grew up in a single-parent home, mostly comprised of women because my mother was always reaching out to help my aunts and her girlfriends who became my GOD aunts. I grew up on welfare. My mother was always working two and sometime three jobs to make ends meet. My grandmother Mildred and grandfather Willie were and are the financial backbone for the family. I grew up in the church at Rust United Methodist Memorial Church on 59th and Carpenter. I accepted GOD in my life at an early age, however, I really didn't know HER or HIM at the time. I believed GOD then because I was taught to believe in GOD. I have two nieces, Quintella and Quilita Reyes (1990-1992) and two nephews, Bobby Deonte Smith and Quinten Dunlap, and a host of family and friends. I am the first in my family to graduate from college having received a Bachelor of Science degree in Business Marketing on June 7, 1992.

I wrote this book initially with no desire for it becoming what it is today. I started writing to obtain and maintain the attention of Tiersa Smith whom I met on April 14, 1994, at singer R. Kelly's Platinum Party at Inta's nightclub. I was so captivated by Tiersa's natural beauty I asked and challenged myself, how can I share time with her without buying her love because I didn't have any money. So my desire to be with her was the rain for my writing seed to grow poetically. I wrote her a 40 - 45 page book entitled "myeboneegyrl." The first poem I wrote was in June 1994 and entitled "hisphace," which describes the turgescence of the gunshot wound to the right side of Lemont's head. However, the rudiments of my writings started for the "Rick Party Show" on 107.5 WGCI-FM in March of 1993 when I created a spoken word positive thought segment now called "phood pha tha souL."

Writing is my escape. It has enabled me to mourn, heal and deal with Lemont's physical transition as well as deal with other issues being a BLAK man in Amerikkka. Writing has introduced me to my other side, my soul, my feminine being. My writings have been my vehicle for me to go into the hell of my soul. It has and is purging my mellow fields from weeds of negative thoughts of myself while at the same time transcending me to mental state of BLAK HEAVEN (next book). My writings stopped me from committing suicide. My writings are raw and pure wataa that refreshes my soul. My writing is Lemont's spirit living through me. It is the sun and the storm of my heart -- my shallow and the deep seas of my thoughts. It has given life, death and rebirth to and of myself. I write the way I write because I was bored writing Standard English. I write words the way they sound. The way it is, and not how it should be. My writings are my heart and soul, the inner me on paper. Ultimately, my writings have given me peace.

Peace'n Luv,

kw≡isi

tha
writt'n
wu7dz
n
this
book
iz
my
7age

RELEASE ANXIETY 2 GAIN EXCELLENCE

phood pha tha souL

urban amerikkka

when you are in the midst of urban amerikkka
don't be skared of ha'
when you sea me on the streets
movin' to the heart of my beat
walkin'
talkin'
to myself
by myself
for the betterment of self
i am not krazy or insane
i am freein' the chains
from my brains
so do not run from me
run to me
bekause i am a poet
and the only thing you have to fear from a poet
is the truth

phrom tha phi7st wa7
n heaven between God and satan
wa7 iz dark Lyke a raven
but even a raven
noz when 2 phlee phrom wa7
and it waz wa7
when kain killed abel
2 b tha messenger of tha spiritual wa7
bekuz wa7
bringz phorth destruktion, howeva without destruktion
U kannot have konstruktion or rekonstrucktion
uv Lyf and though Lyf iz Lost
n this game uv Lyf
should there b a winner and should there b a Lozer…

phrom wa7 n heaven
to wa7 on earth
tha end result of wa7
must b and iz
pes…

howeva, world wa7 III iz on tha
mynd
tha wa7
u must phyte and ovakome everyday
iz tha wa7
within'
self

wu7dz
(7=r)

Lyf
WILL get betta
and i'm not tellin' U this jus' 2 stroke your ego
or 2 make u pheel guud
and it'z all God
i tell u this
with all uv tha wu7dz
i have eva spok'n or writt'n
n
my
Lyf

n'nocent7age

n'nocent7age
hear our children kry
n'nocent7age

yo' i'm tired uv people askin me y i'm n a gang
yeah! i'm a "g"
and i have otha shortiez on tha block who want 2 b Lyke me
ain't nothin' Lyke Luv, respect yeah! and tha phear
i have tha phattest pocketz with tha phreshess gear
yeah i'm n a gang
and so what i slang
my motha all kaught up n her boy phriend and her new job
my phatha n jail doin Lyf bekuz he murdered and robbed
my unclez r "g'z", both my brothaz, hell my sista iz even a "g"
and i'm only fifteen
and this iz what i've seen
and this iz what i know
kryme, karz, money and ho afta ho
my otha "g'z" accept me phor who i am
yeah, i did a phew dryve byez and several kar jackz
hell everybody gotta start somewhere plus my otha "g'z" got my back
and i know my kreed say thou shall not kill or steal
and thou shall honor thou motha and GOD
but ryte now GOD ain't payin' tha billz so, until i phynd a bettaway
i'm a kontinue 2 do it my way
i gotta get myne so i'm a take yourz
oh and about dyin' thats apart uv my Lyf style
phrom urban amerikkka 2 tha suburbz, vyolynz iz heard
from paduca, kentucky to springfield oregon
from edinborough, P-A, 2 jonesboro, A-K
x'skuse me i just gotta page
and kryme iz how i xx'press my …

n'nocent7age
hear our children kry
n'nocent7age

yeah, yeah, yeah
i'm just a young gyrl and i'am about 2 have my third chyld
n'joyin' Lyf havin' much phun bein' buck wyld
one iz 32 and the other iz 37
i Lyke older guyz
they Look guud n their suitz, shirtz, and nyce tiez
my motha strung-out on drugz and i neva met my phatha
welfare goin' take kare uv us so i don't even have 2 botha
one week i had sex everyday with a different guy
jus so my motha kan kontinue 2 get hy
and i don't mynd havin' sex kuz this iz all i sea
when i turn on tha radio or watch tha t.v.
i don't mynd goin' 2 skool but i really don't have no hope for no phuture

4

i do guud n some klazzez but otha klazzez i need a tutor
and tha only thing i really want out uv Lyf iz truly 2 b Luv'd
i'm only six-teen yearz uv age
and sex iz how i xx'press my ...

n'nocent7age
hear our children kry
n'nocent7age

i didn't know my phatha
but i went on 2 central state university anyway so i didn't have 2 botha
with everyday Lyf trialz 'n tribulation
but then kame my kollege graduation
my younger brotha wuz kill'd
but thru my spiritual, mental and physikal n'lytenment i have Learn'd 2 deal
my kousinz wuz kill'd tha same way
two yearz Later on tha same day
but i know itz goin' 2 b alryte kuz i kontinue 2 pray
my otha kousin wuz kill'd n a kar accident
my unkle dyed phrom aids
my great grand motha jus past
and jus tha otha day someone stole my motha'z kar but they didn't get phar
bekuz they ran out uv gas
thru all tha xx'treme challengez and kontroversy i have remain'd n HER ...

thanx U GOD phor givin' me this earthly stage
and thru my poetree sage
i xx'press my ...

n'nocent7age
hear our children kry
n'nocent7age

BLAKMAN
(youngman)

BLAKMAN
where are U today
are U so afraid of Life's challenges that U kontinue to runaway
runnin' away to krime, theft, drugs, drug sellin', violence and the mental and physical
rape of ourselves and our BLAKWOMEN

BLAKMAN
where are U today
when are we goin' to stop killin' and shootin' one anotha
don't we realize we are taking someone's son our brotha

BLAKMAN
where are U today
stop takin' the easy way out
tryin' to be that man with the street
klout

BLAKMAN
where are U today
i to experience the pain and hurt
it seems Like it WILL neva go away
but understand that was yesterday

BLAKMAN
where are U today
physikal slavery has ended over one hundred years ago
now, when WILL you allow yourself to spiritually and mentally grow

BLAKMAN
where are U today
always pointin' the finga blamin' the otha man
BLAKMAN
those of U who are makin' it when WILL you extend that otha hand

BLAKMAN
where are U today
it is jus not about individual needs
when WILL you reach back and plant some positive seeds

BLAKMAN
where are U today
U kan achieve what eva we want out of Life
but when are you goin' to make that sakrafice

sakrafice...stop that gansta mentally
sakrafice...stop pursuin' your dreams for jus money and women
sakrafice...get to know you BLAKMAN

pesnLuv BLAKMAN...pesnLuv BLAKMAN...pesnLuv BLAKMAN

bekause of You i am ... who i am
and You make me ... me
if You hadn't said so ... i WILL not be
          kause i jus wanna be what You want me 2 be
so i kontinue 2 grow in You
but sometimes i want 2 Leave You
so my phamily kan have my several Loafs of bread and few fish
kause my wish
is 2 be with You
but my kuriousity of You
keeps me inYou
bekause i need You
Like the morning needs the sun
and though i kannot see You ... You are not the missin' one
i need You Like the ocean needs the streams
so i dreams
of You bein' the rein in my desert
though at times i have desserted You
You have kept me Like the glow of the nite from the moon
and when there is gloom
in my earth ... your Son shines
on time
and in time
but some time
my mind
is so konvolluted with these earthly things
but wisdom of You is more precious than a diamond 2 be ringed
so You ring
my temple bell
so i tell
othas about You
this is how i keep it true
2 thouself
but You know me betta than i know myself
but i kan't do this by myself
and You told me You were goin' back
and You went back
and You WILL b back
so i kry out 2 You
by writin' 2 You
kause, i need You
Like humans need air
i need You
Like fish need wataa
and through You i kan walk on wataa
and bekause of You i didn't quit a Looooooong time ago
kause i Left my ego
so we go
soarin' Like an eagle
for You and my people

seven seas pluz five great Lakes iz twelve
so i delve
 in2 the depts of my sea
tryin' 2 find BLAK pearls of me
and though at times the pressure from the depts of my sea
does get 2 me
so please, please, please don't Leave me
as i walk this earth in Your universe
your word is bond that You make the Last first
and i know i have succumbed
by tryin' 2 Let otha earths in my hemisphere
but i do have an ear … 2 hear
i admit i am wrong
You have kept me sof'n strong
so i Long
for You in me …

onepluzoneizthree

8

the7evolutionwillbetelevized
(tribute 2 Gil Scott-Heron)

the7evolutionwillbetelevized
kause my eyes
rekongize
the Lies in truthful disguizes
tha7evolutionwillbetelevized

you WILL be able to stay home my brotha
you WILL be able to plug in, turn on and kopout
you WILL be able to Loze ya'self on skag skipout on kommercial breaks
with your 40oz. distilled spirits
kause you ain't trying to hear it
but your eyes WILL realize
the7evolutionwillbetelevized

the 7evolution is bein' televized
from the montell show to harpo
and the summit of teens
but this ain't no bet
kause i'm gramblin' for my mental state to central state

the7evolutionwillbetelevized
from wgci to wlib to ysb -- kause i be
on abc, nbc, cbs, fox, upn, wgn, and cnn
without kommercial interruptions
kause they show all kurruptions
tha7evolutionwillbtelevized

the7evolution will show you pictures
of mayor barry and clinton gettin' hy, 2 white wataa, 2 monica lewinsky,
to clinton blowin' his sax
to the GOP's kontract with amerikkka, to the flat tax
to four star general named colin powell
the7evolution will be Led by a child
and she WILL be a blessin' in disquise
the7evolutionwillbetelevized

the7evolution WILL give you sundance award winnin' stars
larenz tate, nia long and reggie gibson in Love jones
bekause brothas and sistas WILL stop throwin' stones
from angela bassett to denzel washington in Malcolm X
to generation next, to generation x and the x is now known
bekause my eyes realize and recognize the Liez in the truthful disguise
the7evolution will be televized

the7evolution WILL give your mouth sex appeal
the7evolution WILL get rid of the nub
the7evolution WILL make you phat from bein' weak
kause you eat red meat
from them burger joints

the7evolutionwillbetelevized
from a spike lee's joint ... he got game
to cuba gooding jr. ... oscar fame
to soul food by george tillman jr.
kame to you sooner
so, you kan think with your eyes
and realize
the 7evolution is bein' televized my sistas and brothas
there WILL be pictures of Jesse Jackson freein' the POW's
there WILL be pictures of tha o.j. trial
there WILL be pictures of you and ya home boy pushin a stolen kolor tv
  in a shoppin kart down krenshaw boulevard from the riotz in wattz
there WILL be pictures of the police beatin' rodney king on instant replay
there WILL be pictures of the police beatin' rodney king on instant replay
there WILL be pictures of michael jackson bein' run out of hollywood with a
  brand new process and photos of his genitals which were
  taken by tha l-a-p-d synikals
there WILL be pictures of muhammad ali Lighting the olympic torch
and torched were churches by tha kkk's theft
to 2 pac and biggie smalls death
tha7evolutionwillbetelevized

moesha, good news, new york under cover, and parenthood
are revelant to phamily matters, in the house, to be touched by an angel, to malcolm and
eddie
bekause my eyes are ready
and sistas WILL kare that brothas have Left the hood
bekause sistas WILL be in the hood
karin' about all my children
teachin' them some betta ways
for some betta days
to sea with their minds eye to realize
tha7evolutionwillbetelevized...

there WILL be hylytes on the 10 0'klock news of hillary rodham clinton
winnin' a grammy for an afrikan proverb
"it takes a village to raize our children"
to Liberationist ellan degeneres komin' out that she is gay
to the wnba
the theme song WILL be sung
by babyphace, r. kelly, kirk phranklin, blackstreet, maxwell, eric benett, kenny Lattimore
and written' by sonia sanchez, maya angelou, gwendolyn brooks, nikki giovani, kim
ransom, buddha bless, von, prosperity and jessica care moore
kause my eyes kare more
to recognize
the7evolutionwillbetelevized

the7evolution WILL be right back afta these messages
about white tornados, white hurrikanes, and white people
WILL be apart of the solution and the7evolution
the7evolution WILL go guud with wataa to give you that natural surge
but Let me diverge

to help you unmask your eyes
so you WILL realize
the 7evolution is bein' televized

the 7evolution WILL phyte germs that kause bad breathe
the 7evolution WILL put you in a four wheel drive
the 7evolution WILL be Live
from the wear of 7age, to guud morning afro amerikka, to a bad moon risin'
to primetime, juwan howard and emmitt smith
from uptown to downtown
from the suburbs to the hoods
from allen iverson, kevin garnett, kobe bryant, to tiger woods
these spok'nwu7dz are public enemy #1
kause knowledge reigns supreme over everyone
kause i bring d-knowledge to tha brain
makin' reg e. gaines
and this generation is tribe kalled kwest
we have mo' zeal than zest
the7evolution is bein' televized
the7evolutionwillbetelevized

from hip hopera, jazz, reggae, alternative rock to hip hop
these spok'nwu7dz won't stop Like reign dropz
i taught i told you that we won't stopp!
i taught i told you that we won't stopp!
bekause my eyes
realize and WILLunmask the Liez
in the truthful disguise

the7evolutionwillbetelevized
the7evolutionwillbetelevized
the7evolutionwillbetelevized
the7evolutionwillbetelevized

the7evolutionwillbe no re-runs, my sistas and brothas

the7evolutionwillbe LYVE!

change

sum uv us
base our opulence on tha change
we have n our akkountz
but don't akkount
pha change
that we need a change
change n mynd
change n heart
change n attitude
change WILL help your altitude
change n Lyf
change n konversation
change … change … change
and i may only have 585 changes
n my akkount
but i akkount
pha change
kuz i have changed
my wayz
Lyke dayz
and i change
a million attitudes weekly
though i stay meekly
on gci
no need 2 ask y
but u change
Lyke sekondz on tyme'n
and u b myn'n
tha deepest depthz uv ya mental state
2 central state
kuz your state
uv mynd needz 2
change
i givez
change
Lyke tyme
kuz i have mo'
change
then the sandz
what upz sandz of the sea shorez
open doorz
Lyke bell boyz
but i b a bad boy 2
i b tru
2 this
change

n make'n tha ryte choice
when u know your background
kuz tha ground u walk on won't Let u turn your back
on yourself most uv all your people
but we make this a sekond hand sequel
thinkin' our konflitz are krucial
so we thro anotha tantrum
kuz we won't change
but most uv all we want presidential change
so we WILL Lye, cheat, steal and deceive
2 achieve
but now we have 2
      make tha ryte choice
for change
bekuz armageddon iz here
bekuz i'ma gettin' tired uv b-n tired
so
      make tha ryte choice
guud ova bad
sad 2 glad
phrom tha surburbz 2 tha hoodz
phrom drugz 2 hugz
phor more pes n Luv
bekuz b-4 tha end u need 2 know what syde
r u goin' 2 be on
northsyde
eastsyde
westsyde
southsyde
homisyde
genisyde
suisyde
GODsyde
and my spok'n wu7dz WILL make ya head nod
phrom syde 2 syde
so with ya' aktion and your voice
konsistantly
      make tha ryte choice

Motha'z day

Motha'z day
there r not enuff wu7dz n tha human Language that i kan say
though these wu7dz r phew
they r tru
uv U
kuz your Luv
iz an unkonditional Luv
it'z a GOD'z Luv
and Motha'z Luv iz sweet potato pye
no need 2 ask y
bekuz regardless uv tha situation
there iz no Limitation or hestitation
n u havin' my back
and u have back
even when U r n phront uv me
so this makez U regal
and this iz tha sequal
there r not enuff wu7dz n tha human Language that i kan say
otha than

Happy ... Happy ... Motha'z day

Phatha'z day

Phatha'z day
there are many thingz i kan say
on this pesful and grand day
bekuz there are a great number of men
who take responsibility for their responsibilities
and i am not jus my babiez daddy
i protect my phamily Lyke the sand iz a barrier to tha sea
i provide for my phamily Lyke the earth provides for the x'istance uv Lyf
and my wyf
i have her back Lyke spring 2 summa
not taken her for granted
my sun shynes only on her planet
kuz GOD resyde
so i fertilize her syde
with sekond on tyme'n
and i share tha dyn'n
my several Loafz uv bread and my phew persh
i Luv my wyf and children Lyke tha PRINCE uv PES Luv'z tha church
i am a man who iz strong 'n sof'n
i am here often
phor my son as i play katch n tha backyard
and take my daughters for walkz
teaching them their abc'z
and thru me my children WILL believe and achieve
their dreamz n Lyf
bekuz every day i sakrafyce
my Lyf phor their Lyf
and this day and everyday

Happy … Happy … Happy

Phatha'z day

hisphace

tha ryte syde uv his head had a whole in it tha syze uv a grape phruit
hisphace
tha ear on tha ryte syde of his head wuz barely attached
hisphace
his eyez were steel open they had bulged out uv his head and his head had bekame
disphigur'd from tha gun shot blast
hisphace
blood had ran phrom his noze to his mouth whyle blood on the morgue table
wuz n puddlez phrom tha head wound
hisphace
LEMONT didn't even Look Lyke him
hisphace
only if u kould sea
hisphace…hisphace…hisphace

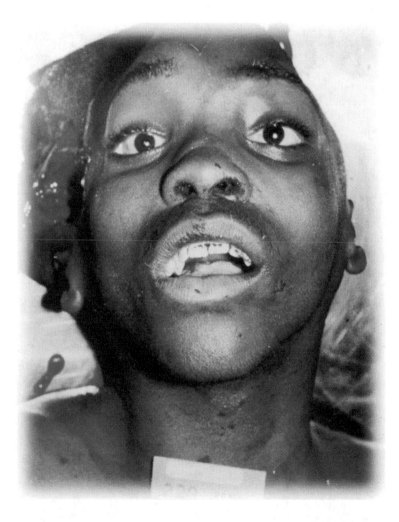

thaLetters

October 26, 1995

Eric, what's up bra? I am kweisi. I am writing you this letter because I would like to meet and forgive you for the murder of my younger brother James Lemar Ford. During our meeting if you choose, you do not have to say or admit anything. I would just like the opportunity to express my personal and phamily pain and hurt. And in turn, make peace with you.

I pray for you and your phamily that you are doing well under your konditions. I also pray and hope you accept my invitation. I want to do this for myself so, I kan end the chapter on Lemont's death and move on progressively with my life. Also, for my kontinual personal healing and to let you know it's o.k. That I understand your pain and struggle as a young BLAK male in this society. Please gives us the opportunity to meet and perhaps we may be able to develop a relationship where I kan help you during your tumultuous times.

Sincerely,

kweisi

P.S.   If you accept this invitation feel free to kall me collect at....

17

Johnathan, what's up bra? I am kweisi. I am writing you this letter because I would like to meet and forgive you for the murder of my younger brother James Lemar Ford. During our meeting if you choose, you do not have to say or admit anything. I would just like the opportunity to express my personal and phamily pain and hurt. And inturn, make peace with you.

I pray for you and your phamily that you are doing well under your konditions. I also pray and hope you accept my invitation. I want to do this for myself so I kan end the chapter on Lemont's death and move on progressively with my life. Also, for my kontinual personal healing and to let you know it's o.k. That I understand your pain and struggle as a young BLAK male in this society. Please gives us the opportunity to meet and perhaps we may be able to develop a relationship where I kan help you during your tumultuous times.

Sincerely,

kweisi

P.S.   If you accept this invitation feel free to kall me collect at….

November 6, 1995

Johnathan, what's up bra? I received your attempt to kall me via my messages on my answering service, unfortunately I was not here. Please try to kall again Thursday morning if possible. I was very excited that you had kalled, because that gives us a sign of hope that you and I kan reconcile. However, if you are not able to kall on Thursday please keep trying and if we don't have the opportunity to meet soon Johnathan, I want you to know I DO FORGIVE YOU BRA and I will kontinue to pray for you and your phamily.

pesnluv,

kweisi

P.S.   kall

P.P.S. Eric hasn't kalled yet but if you see him, talk to him and let him know it's
        o.k.

November 6, 1995

Eric, what's up bra? This is kweisi writing you again. I don't know if you attempted to kall yet but if not please kall Thursday morning. If I am not here try again. I understand you may not have kome to make peace with yourself but I know it is within you so, you and I kan make peace. However, we will do this per se you agree at or on your time and if there is a possibility that you do not want us to meet. Eric, I want you to know that I DO FORGIVE YOU BRA and I will kontinue to pray for your phamily. Oh yeah, Johnathan did kall but I was not here. I was very excited that he had kalled. Bra please kall at your konvience.

pesnLuv,

kweisi

P.S.   kall

whatkanikeep

if
i
kan't
keep
my
wu7d,
what
kan
i
keep

ithankU

U have shown me
so much grace and mercy
i hear and Sea
tha phruitz uv my Labor
so i savor
tha taste uv success and phailya
so i tell ya
nyne tymez and it ain't enuff
U blessed me with my spok'n wu7dz
iz tha ryte stuff...

ithankU

make-up & photo by Prosperity

boogieman. . . . . . . boogieman. . . . . . . .boogieman

alwayz kallin' me thaboogieman
or r u jus skar'd uv me man
alwayz kallin' me thaboogiman
or du u jus phear me man

kallin' me thaboogieman
alwayz usin' me az your x'skapegoat
knowin u kill'd ol'gyrl and slit ol'boyz throat

kallin' me thaboogieman
i should b tha one runnin' man
Lyke killin' your wyf and unborn chyld
pha some paper u kan't even wryte on, damn that'z wyld

kallin' me thaboogieman
and susan drove her kidz n tha riva
doin' that dumb shhhhhhh! WILL make a dead man shiva

kallin' me thabooigeman
u promoted the death uv yummie world wyde and on klock magazine
what about that whyte boy who shot that store owner dead on tha scene

kallin' me thaboogieman
tryin' 2 manipulate my mental anatomy
and that otha whyte boy who shot his phriend bekuz he didn't accept his otha phriend
apology

kallin' me thaboogieman
whyte amerikkka kan't keep all uv BLAK amerikka down
so when will u kome around
kuz alot uv us use our myndz
but u wont promote that kind
thinkin' i'm jus guud when i am playin' ball
and that million man and million woman's march we did walk tall

kallin' me thaboogieman
the media has shown me 2 think uv myself as inferior
i must use my mynd to show myself superior

kallin' me thaboogieman
yeah, yeah i must admit brothaz have komitt'd homisyde afta homisyde
but u know what u r doin' so u steel ain't justiphyd

kallin' me thaboogieman
usin' tha media 2 keep me n mayhem
phrom tha radio 2 tha tv it'z all jus a skam

kallin' me thabooigeman
alwayz pointin' tha phinga 2 my huud
kuz whyte amerikka is alwayz up 2 know guud

kallin' me thaboogieman
u were that one who n'slaved me man
killin' millionz uv BLAKZ man

kallin' me thaboogieman
u r tha one who is real wick'd man
plotin' out malcolm x daughter man
2 take out farrakhan man

kallin' me thaboogieman
and hitler kill'd more than six million man

kallin' me thaboogieman
and thoze brothaz who kill'd their own parentz man

kallin' me thaboogieman
and ol' boy n kaliphornia took that army tank man

kallin' me thaboogieman
and ol' boy in phlorida kid-napped them handikap kidz man

kallin' me thaboogieman
what about waco man

kallin' me thaboogieman
what about thoze montanamenz man

kallin' me thaboogieman
what about tha unibomber man

kallin' me thaboogieman
jeffery wuz eatin' me man

kallin' me thaboogieman
and tha divided placez blew up that building n oklahoma man
now u r usin' those guyz az pattsiez man

kallin' me thaboogieman
and those guyz who wear whyte suitz 2 burn up krossez and BLAK churches man

kallin' me thaboogieman
it wuz a whyte male who bomb'd the nynty-six olympikz man

kallin' me thaboogieman
what about thoze three white malez who try'd 2 rob that bank n san diego man

kallin' me thaboogieman
what about that mazz suisyde n san diego man

kallin' me thaboogieman
what about that whyte male who drove around tha kountry n kill'd that phasion designer
man

kallin' me thaboogieman
what about that whyte male n texas who drug that brotha from tha back uv his truck man

kallin' me thaboogieman
and that teacher who raped her student man

kallin' me thaboogieman
what about thoze 2 boyz n jonesboro, arkansa man

kallin' me thaboogieman
what about that whyte male who shot up the state kapital building man

kallin' me thaboogieman
what about those 2 whyte males in wyoming man who killed that otha white male bekuz
he wuz gay man

kallin' me thaboogieman
u r tha one who iz real skary man

kallin' me thaboogieman
i should b phearin' u man

kallin' me thaboogieman
kuz i'm an n'tellektual man

kallin' me thaboogieman
bekuz u know i'm thabettaman

i kanwalkonwataa

i kan walk on wataa
kan u walk on wataa
well, u believe u kan phly
so ask ya'self y
how kan u believe n GOD whom u neva
seen
and not believe n ya'self who u sea
everyday
u need 2 pray
phor ya' souL
kus this iz phood pha tha souL
        phood pha the souL
             pha tha souL
kuz
i kan walk on wataa
by makin' pes and keepin' pes
with my G'zus pes
who iz tha PRINCE uv PES
and b n Lyke HIM
i kan take tha whole world on
by holdin' on … Lyke tha SUN
kuz
i kan walk on wataa
thru my PHATHA and the stormz uv tha
sea
don't botha me
so u myte think i'm heartless
there fore u kall me hopeless
but tha deepa i delve n 2 tha sea
tha betta i get 2 know me
bekuz sometymez, sometymez r. kelly
i kan't sea it
but i steel must believe it
2 b it
and there iz something 2 it
bekuz phaith without work iz dead
so n my head
i steel must konceive it
if i kan't sea it
and take tha phirst stepz 2 achieve it
bekuz b 4 i know GOD
i phirst must know thou self

so i question myself
how kan i believe n GOD whom i neva
seen
and not believe n myself who i sea
everyday
so i kontinue 2 pray

phor tha rain
az it rain
and i kan stand tha rain
but now that tha rain iz gone
 i kan sea klearly now
so i WILL regin
on tha earth Lyke tha wataaz n noah's
dayz
and nowadayz
i'm openin up tha red sea
and makin' my x'odus so u kan sea …
me
thru tha PRINCE uv PES
that
i kan walk on wataa

phyve'nhalfyearz

on one day
january eighteen nyneteen hundred and nynety-two
tha phamily buried U
it haz taken me
two thousand dayz on june twenty-phift, nyneteen hundred nynety-seven
2 bury U
i buried U
n my dreamz

i wuz talkin' 2 my wyf
oopz she'z not my wyf…yet but it phirst startz n tha mynd
so n kynd
i apologyze phor misleadin' tha witness
but she phitz this
deskription similitude 2 my motha
and i'm goin' 2 Luv ha
Lyke tha PRINCE uv PES Luv'd tha church
with my several Loafz uv bread and my phew perch
we were havin' koversation about sharing hugz
and i wuz x'plannin' this iz how i show my Luv
2 a person
without tellin' a person
and she wuz sayin' a person
kan take that tha wrong way
and i agreed but both man and woman even i need a hug phrom day 2 day
she said, "i am jus spoil'd and that i am a momma'z boy"
yeah, i am a momma'z boy
"well that'z where U go 2 get your hugz phrom your momma…boy"
bekuz these women don't Luv u
they Luv your work bekuz they don't know u 2 Luv u"
and that myte b tru
but a hug
iz how i sho my Luv
phor my people
and 2 my people
az i garden my earth
but my gyrl gave rebirth…2 my deepest thoughtz
so i start'd delvin' n2 me
asking myself y do i really hug people
and n tha past several dayz i had been dreaming about LEMONT
and jus afta awakenin' phrom a dream about LEMONT
it wuz a dream uv some phriendz and myself burying LEMONT
and u may ask what doez this have 2 do with
myLastHUG
well this haz everything 2 do with myLastHUG
bekuz out uv all tha tha tymez LEMONT and i Left each otha
we Left each otha with a hug
on December 27, 1991 that Last tyme i saw LEMONT alive
we didn't hug
so tha hug that i share with U
iz
myLastHUG
LEMONT and i didn't share

(I got myLastHUG 11.11.98 in a dream that I had of LEMONT at the bottom of the sea)

n 1969 i wuz born on a kollege kampus
so u kan stamp this
but don't kramp this
style
kuz i have more style and klazz
than a designerz phasion skool
so sta-n-skool 2 b kool … now that'z kool
though i am at tha rudiment uv my journey
and on my journey my goal iz 2 pheel n that generationgap
phrom tha baby boom generation
2 generation x
2 generation nex
2 generation y
2 generation now
kuz now i must have an image uv substance and essence
along with klazz, style'n elegance
Lyf iz a gift that'z y itz a present
and this iz a phakt
my spok'n wu7dz WILL make ya' souL klap
so u pheel n tha
generation...

(woman's voice)
 x'skuze me may i karry your bookz.

i 2 thought tha grazz wuz greena on tha otha syde
oshen tyde
brushed up against tha same syde
on rough terrain
n my soul it rained
pha dayz
my wayz
Led me n2 me
but out uv me
kame
shame
i tried 2 wash it away phrom my earth
but u kan't wash away
what happened yesterday
n my bored'm
i got with shem
and i just Left a moon
that wanted my sunshyne 2 make ha' phull n tha nyte
but i wuz n tha twilyte
uv my kuriousity
which killed this kat
out uv one Lyf
eight Left 2 get it ryte
my syte
that iz n
i must begin
ova
i must think with tha head on my shoulda
bekuz on tha otha syde it iz much kolda
i have Learned 2 wataa my grazz 2 keep it greena so i don't krossova
2 tha otha syde pha a whem
with shem

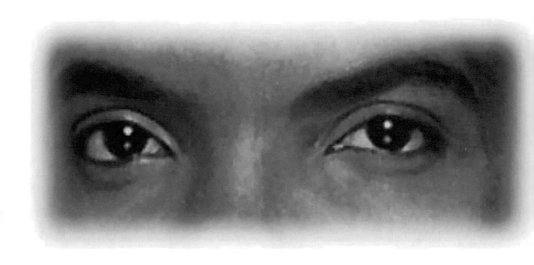

n'nervizchen

n'nervizchen
mi n'nervizchen haz me delvin' n 2 tha deptz uv mi sea
i need n'nervizchen 2 sea
that one pluz one iz three
my mynd, my body, thru my n'nervizchen i sea my souL
tha one who iz most Hy, knowz tha path i take az i kome phorth pure az gold
kourageous 'n bold
mi n'nervizchen iz Lyke tha wataaz uv Lake michigan kold
kold 2 kool my ninety-eight point six degreez on a hot summer day
mi n'nervizhen iz bittersweet Lyke Lemonade

(tribute 2 BLAK HEAVEN)

i saw your phace phrom tha rephlektion n thawyndeau
and though
your roze iz planted n parsh phieldz
i steel
win though
and tha glow … phrom your smyle upon your phace
i had 2 m'brace
az my eyez kanvas'd your phace
az thirty-nyne sharez tha place
by your syde
but n syde
uv me
my BLAK wataaz ripple n my sea uv emochenz
my PHATHA has bless'd me 2 sea your devochen
but r U happee
on my train ryde no need 2 part thee
az U depart
your roze WILL alwayz be plant'd n tha heart uv my mellow pheelz
as i ascend 2
BLAK HEAVEN
though with U i have road
tha7edLyneuvemochenz

phreedom

phreedom iz doin' what U Luv 2 do
phreedom iz b-n tru … 2 U
phreedom iz phacin' ya phearz
phreedom it sometymez takez yearz
phreedom WILL have U rejoice thru ya tearz
phreedom iz b-n able 2 submitt 2 anotha
phreedom iz 2 Luv ya sista and ya' brotha
phreedom iz 2 x'prezz ya self without harmin' no one else
phreedom kan Lock U up
        U kan b Lock'd up n phreedom
phreedom iz b-n a spiritual slave phor tha kreator
        U kan kreate your phreedom
      by kontrolling tha events n ya Lyf
      n'dependence iz
phreedom

phyte

i phyte with my spok'n wu7dz
tha misedukation uv tha negro
steel have boyz that r bad komin' thru tha mental back doe
tha psychological vul and tha zid
u r silly goat kidz
with your mental shallow wu7dz and radio skitz
stick 2 playin' tha hitz
and phood pha tha soul hitz
tha souL 2 edukate
though it u try 2 desekrate
u put me n 7age i must Let it out tha hate
uv tha angle uv Lyte that shynez thru u
i phorgive u ... seventy tymez seven, kuz u know not what u do
u n'ntellektual juvenyle
u kouldn't sail akrozz tha world or tha nile
n a six hundred thousandz ton oil tanka
so i must shank...ya...chainz
phrom ya brainz
kuz my n'ner me
phyte'z
tha n'amee
2 L'evate ya' myndz Lyke wataa
so boyz who r bad kan bekome one with wataa
my spok'n wu7dz iz my plyte
with them i
phyte

happeeness

happeeness iz havin' a relationship with tha most Hy
happeeness iz phood pha tha souL on gci
happeeness iz Luv and support phrom tha phamily nest
happeeness iz b-n U at your best
happeeness iz health
happeeness iz self wealth
happeeness is monetary wealth
      kuz money answerz n a phyiskal world all thingz
happeeness is 2 pknow y tha kaged bird singz
happeeness iz 2 do what U Luv 2 do whether u get paid or not
happeeness iz b-n ninety-eight point six degreez hot
happeeness iz 2 do what U Luv 2 do phor phree and n tyme, on
      tyme and n due tyme U WILL get paid
happeeness iz a kool-aid … smyle
happeeness iz b-n a babe n tha wyld
happeeness iz 2 share your Luv and tyme
happeeness iz 2 reproduce a positive vybe Lyke the number nyne
      U r my phriend
      b-n my phriend
      iz
happeeness

Livnikka

(tribute 2 The Last Poets)

r u a
nikka
thinkin' itz kool 2 b dumb
yet when europeanz n'slaved us
they kill'd us
when we Learn'd or kut off our handz when we play'd the drumz
u not knowin' your past u sta mentally sikka
it keepz u an ignorant nikka

u nikka
u steal this and kar jack that
tryin's 2 keep ya pocketz phat
thinkin' u kool
yet u keep ya people n the sesspool
uv drugz and kryme
but with tyme
and n tyme
u gone do tyme
b-hynd barz or n dirt
kuz u phlert
with tha trikka
u jus anotha street nikka

u nikka
u use your silhouette
2 keep brothaz n check
tryin' 2 get
starlet
quikka
u r jus a harlot uv a nikka

u nikka
u Left tha hood
pha hollywood
staightin' ya' hair
and bleachin' ya skin
and u steel don't even phit-n
now i wonder how iz ya mental
afta they treat'd u Lyke a kriminal
tak'n photoz uv ya genitalz
and tha sad part about it iz u jus don't phikka
they're playin' u phor anotha hollywood nikka

u nikka
u have mov'd 2 tha surburbz and bekame middle klazz
with no klazz
with your degree, md or phd
yet tha dyshkee

u have on
wuz mad n taiwan
u misedukat'd nikka

u nikka
he keepz u n mental shallow wataaz
kuz he slaughterz
ya mynd
by keepin' ya spiritually b-hynd
n this physikal world
tellin' u it'z all about tha karz, klothez and tha gyrlz
and he really ain't your phriend
tellin u itz all about tha benjamenz
kuz his endz
meet
i will steel humble myself 2 wash his feet
2 set an example quikka
he iz jus a sample nikka

u nikka
who work n a hy ryze
tell Lyzez n truthful disguizez
with your two and three piece suit
makin' your Loot
off uv your kynd
not usin' your mynd
n your psylyns
have us drinkin' vyolence
sellin' us BLAKZ, Latinos, Mexicans, Puerto Ricans malt Likka
steppin' on your brotha kuz u want 2 get yourz quikka
u r a korporate nikka

u nikka
who go 2 church every sunday
and bible klazz on wedensday
yet tha only tyme u pray
iz when situationz r bad
u have been had
by tha angel uv Lyte
u steel rephuse 2 sea tha Lyte
n self
u have worldly wealth
but spiritually po kuz u don't Listen
HE did not say HE wuz a kristian
HE said iz tha truth, tha way, tha Lyf
u steel don't sakrafyce
thinkin' it iz hod
but u r tha essence uv GOD
but u jus don't phikka
u r a religious nikka

u nikka
or wikka
u get your breast, butt and Lipz thick
kuz, u wanna b a nikka quick
yet u won't give me no kredit for my n'ventions
yet u steel tryin' 2 phigga out how benjamen banneker draft'd d.c. 2 sharp precision
and what eva i do n my rehearsals
iz bound 2 b n your kommercials
tryin' 2 b hip with no hop
u need 2 stop
kuz u2 talk slang
so whats' up with that thang
yet u judge me bekuz uv tha komplextion uv my skin
yet u sit-n
tha sun
phor some
komplektion n your skin 2 tan quikka
u wanna b a nikka

nikka dye
dye nikka
nikka dye
so tha real nikkaz
not
igorant
knowin'
knowledge uv
ancestorz
kan take ova

m'ptekonversation

upon my seat on tha "L"
my earz phell
on a konversation that wuz m'pte
and it simply
were tha wu7dz uv simple wayz
didn't phaze
tha sista who wuz tha receivee
jus want'd a pes treaty
phrom her phriendz
didn't want tha relationship 2 end...

meet
they sat back n their seat
with m'ptekonversation
goin' back 'n phorth - phorth'n back
about this brotha who keep this sista on her back
az i kontinu'd 2 Listen 2 my steel and quiet voice
my choice
uv wu7dz
that i heard
wuz that their konversation
pheel'd tha pagez
uv my
m'ptekonveration

b-e-t
wegotit
showz with substance and essence
phrom tha past 2 tha presence
so make tha ryte choicez
and have an ear 2 hear our voicez
phrom benson
wegotit
phor tha n'tellektz who Lyke 2 phlex as U walk
b-e-t talk
phrom viewz uv a komik
wegotit
2 b-e-t nuz
wegotit
phrom tha summit uv teenz 2 a city tha will make u wrap
b-e-t makez ya'souL klap
wegotit
phrom video vybrationz
there iz no limitationz
uv tha groovez phrom tha b-e- t planet
so don't take my spok'n wu7dz phor granet
b-e-t
wegotit

i watch theze two young brothaz get on tha bus
no phus
jus a Little Luv phrom tha older brotha
az he helpz his younger brotha
2 his seat
so he kan rest his pheat
az they dangle phrom his seat
and within sekondz tha younder brotha wuz asleep
on his brothaz Lap
i tell U tha truth it made my souL klap
2 watch tha hapz
az tha older brotha gaze'd upon hisphace
he show'd his Luv, mercy and his grace
n tha guud nuz i had 2 ponder
tha oldest brotha WILL alwayz serve the younger
az he slept
tha older brotha kept … watch ova him
i wish i wuz them
watching them
i had 2 remininsce
i do miss
tha tyme LEMONT and i shar'd
n tha dawn uv an evening and tha day uv Lyte
ikeepmybrotha
n my vizchenz n tha nyte

stopthakkk

sea glossary

Race Kard

every body thought johnny cochran played the race kard
but the media played it real hard
showin' the difference yet indifference
on how BLAKZ and whytez responded to the acquittal
doin' their job to keep us separated from the right to the Left
and straight down the middle
playing hard that race kard

and why didn't the media show
the BLAKZ that believed he did it
and the whytez who agreed he should have been acquitted

however, the media wants to keep us divided
kause they ain't tryin' to provide it…

or us
with no signs of jus us
playin' hard
that race kard
and they have been keeping us separated from day one
because they don't want us to have 20/20 vision
and always stereotyping BLAK males and giving us a "Hard Copy"
knowing the evidence in the o. j. trial was real sloppy
and now tha trial is on tape three kopies of 60 minutes
and the media knows who was involved in it
playin' hard
that race kard
and somebody was making extra money
and the court trial was real funny
playing hard that race kard
and this is supposed to be the Land of Liberty

Luv

a Lot of us are miskonstrued about
Luv
thinking it is a feeling or an emotion
Luv
is a never-ending devotion…like
Luv
between a parent and a child something that Last 'til infinity
Luv
is to disagree but still to be friends with me
Luv
you can choose to share it or not
Luv
how can you give something you never got
Luv
is to give altruism to your fellowman
Luv
is not just doing it when it benefits you and you extended your other hand
Luv is a state of mind
Luv
is a conscious decision to give despite your emotions of another kind
Luv
so Luv and be Luved
tyme is Luv
U r Luv
the divine spirit in U is Luv

i tell u tha truth
u need 2 get 2 tha 7ootz
uv your problemz
by gettin' 2 tha 7ootz
u WILL solve 'em
Lyke tha unseen n tha garden uv eden
it wuz tha serpent that kuz'd tha eatin'
his or her Lyez on tha surphace
kuz him or her 2 surphace
on his or her belly whyle on tha earth
tha 7ootz ... uv my wu7dz WILL give your souL rebirth
kuz u have been sold
Lyez n truthful disquizez
phrom blond hair 2 blu eyez
and this iz not tha nektar uv tha phruitz
so Let me take u 2 tha 7ootz

tha 7ootz
uv your b-n
and though u b-n a kolor uv skin
i steel, i steel must take u 2 tha essense uv your b-n
kuz u r b-n blynd
phrom ya eyez 2 ya mynd
kuz u kan't hate the 7ootz
and Luv tha phruitz
uv your Loot
so Let me boot ... tha city uv ya m'agination
and this is not tha pigment uv my m'agination
phrom tha nationz
uv egypt, ghana and kenya
afrika iz steel n ya
at tha 7ootz
afrikan'z were tha phirst 2 wear butta hairstylez n tha trybez
so here'z tha vybe
phrom women 2 men
our hairstylez wyn
kuz when women wore certain stylez uv braidz 2 x'press
that she wuz single
kuz she wanted 2 mingle
or if she were n mourning or tha morning she celebrated tha birth
uv her phirst chyld
her hairstyle also x'press her social rank
take this 2 the 7ootz uv ya mental bank
anotha trybez sistaz wore their hair n Length
2 x'press their strenght
2 otha sista kuttin' their hair 2 dryve out evil spiritz
so hear it
though europeanz take kredit for tha french roll they rob'd

tha bob
but we got kobz
kuz we kreat'd tha twist, ringletz, plaitz and tha Locks
and Lyke tha Lox
tha monee, power and respekt iz n tha n'tellekt style uv your hair
phrom a barber's phlair
Lyke khabir's sharp shearz
2 walt'z
kutz add phlavor Lyke malt'z
phrom phadez 2 braids
2 afroz
a brotha knowz … his glory iz n hair that iz gray
so don't stray … away
phrom tha essence uv ya hair b-n
kurly, straight, nok nyne, short or n Length
your hair x'press your spirtual, mental, physikal, social
and ekonomik strength
kuz all treez that bare guud phruitz
have Luv'n deep
rootz

HATE

u WILL neva understand hatred until u hate
tha onez u Luv tha most ...

i hated my own people
i hated my phamily
i hated my motha
i hated BLAK women
tha person i hated tha most afta LEMONT made his transition
          wuz myself ...

n hatred
there iz
Luv

godshotme …

i got shot
n my vizchenz n tha nyte
my spiritual n 'syte
rekognized tha plyte
uv my WILL
so thaboogieman had 2 kill
tha phear n my head
with Lead
az i drove n a parade with tha top down
i got shot down …
godshotme

as i kontinue 2 watch my vizchen
with wataa precision
thaboogieman
had 2 depart
hatred, anger and bittaness phrom my heart
it stopp'd
when i got shot
godshotme

i wuz playin' phootball with my boyz
n tha wyld…wyld hundredz
n tha hood
on my blox
i got rox … by
thaboogieman
n tha HIP
i tried 2 chase
but it wuz n my waist
i kould only HOP
i got shot
godshotme

it wuz tha sleep n my m'agination
i wuz speakin' tha guud newz 2 many nationz
and jacqulyn had my pheet
which Led me 2 meet
BLAK HEAVEN
Little boyz about seven
gettin' their pheet sized phor tha gospel uv pes
az i now rest n pes
b-n one shot away
godshotme …   Ephesian 6:11-17

49

Leftme

when i saw your phace Last nyte
az i wuz goin' 2 sleep

when i saw your phace, when tha shadow uv tha sun wuz steel present
and u r definitely a present
your phace wuz phull
and your glow Lit up tha room
and az i klos'd my iii'z 2 rest
u set ova me n tha southwest
n tha morning
and though i wuz n mourning
tha shadow uv tha sun wuz steel present
it brought joy phrom tha deptz uv my steel BLAK sea
2 sea
your phull vybriant phace
n tha shallowz uv outer space
and the sun place
on your phace
wuz as tha phall
uv tha Leavez n tha phall
and i jus admir'd u phrom aphar
aphar i am steel admirn' u
bekuz u
r so n'dependent
yet dependent on tha one
tha one star that iz tha nukleus uv tha universe
and as i wuz drivin'
i wuz wondering if i would eva see your beautiful phace again
and your vybriant phace
Leftme

Death

death
we all experience
death
sometymez or another
death
az we konsciosly know it iz when someone dyez
but it's jus not then we must realyze
death
happenz every sekond, every minute, every hour, every day
its' when it happenz unexpectedly we begin 2 pray
death
izn't
death
when someone dyez and goez on 2 GOD's way
death
iz also thoze uv us who don't 'njoy Lyf all work and no play

phruitzuvLyf

Lies in truthful disquises
is how the skiii blue
pskno white
and sea red, get in your head
2 vandalize
so i realize
2 bekareful who i say i am, you are
bekause the star
of fifty
is thrifty
in how it obtained its Liberty
by the rapture of this Land from the indigenous people
2 the sequal
of Hiroshima, 2 the project of Tuskegee men of air
kould not bare
the phruitz, tied a rope around a movement that was civil
bekause every time a Son rise
you vandalize
and you don't utilize
the kurrency that is exchanged domestikally 2 feed the Less home
it romed
in 2 paesoes
i am the first generation that kannot pray so
in the institution of Learning
my souL of the sun burnin'
for the PES of a PRINCE
times are intense
by the wrongs
my writin's keeps me strong
2 sta-ryte
my spiritual insyte
is not brutalized
through my spok'nwu7dz
the
phruitzuvLyf
is what i utilize
2 vandalize
negative thoughts of
me

everything n Lyf iz mathmaticz
and tha hyest number n math iz
nyne
and
nyne
iz a GOD's number
GOD iz about reproduktion
and tha number
nyne
iz tha only number that reproducez itself
phrom
zero 2 nyne
one pluz eight iz nyne
two pluz seven iz nyne
three pluz six iz nyne
phour pluz phyve iz nyne
phyve pluz phour iz nyne
six pluz six plus six iz eighteen, one pluz eight iz nyne
9x2 iz 18, 6x3 iz 18, 9x3 iz 27
two pluz seven iz nyne
9x4 iz 36, 9x9 iz 81,
eight pluz one iz nyne
u c, tha phlesh
givez birth 2 tha phlesh
but tha spirit givez birth 2 tha spirit
my mynd shynez Lyke sunshyne
my mynd
iz my
nyne

pesnluv 2 u
i L'evate' myndz Lyke wataa
i kan walk on wataa
bekuz i am bein' and bekomin' one with wataa
2 u wataa
may jus b wataa
but wataa
iz tha essence uv Lyf
and all Lyf
startz n wataa
u kan Liv without bread
but u kan't Liv without wataa
tha earth has been n x'sistance phor ova phyv billion yearz
before God kreat'd tha earth He kreated wataa
tha earth'z surface iz made up uv 141,055,400 square mylez uv wataa
thatz 75% of tha earth
u r uv tha earth
your body makez up 75% uv wataa
tha phountain uv youth iz n wataa
tha phirst thing that phlowz on a women prior 2 birth iz her wataa
wataa komez down wet goez up dry
wataa iz Lyf'n death
wataa iz alwayz movin'
wataa iz alwayz wet
and yet
wataa kan hold a 600,000 oil tanka
and a pebble WILL sanka n wataa
wataa iz shallow
wataa iz deep
tha deepa u go n wataa
tha moore prezzure it iz… kan u handle tha pressure phrom your deep
wataa iz rephreshing 2 tha mynd, body 'n souL
now that u know wataa
here'z your klean glazz uv
wataa

n'nocent7age

Liv, Luv, Laff 'n' Learn

i do, u do

(tribute 2 joseph)

az i set on tha back uv tha bus
i jus
Listened 2 tha voicez uv tha unheard
and i wuz disturb'd
ova tha phus
uv this one partikular voice
bekuz his choice
uv wu7dz where that uv anotha
brotha
i myte add
and this brotha iz a boy who iz bad
and this young brotha
had taken n phrom his souL tha wu7dz
it'z all about tha benjamenz
u sea young people r n'phluenced by what they hear and sea
so if u r not saying or doing anything ryteous
u myte jus
need 2 delve n2 your sea that iz BLAK
and deal phrom within tha n'amee
and add tha missin' 'e' 2 phred
so u don't b misled or mislead
a generation uv young people
bekuz
i do…
what
u`do

WhenrUkomin'BAK

i have read and heard so many spok'n wu7dz about U
but phor some reason
doin' that phall uv tha season
i steel doubt'd U
that U kan walk on watta
and your spok'n wu7dz L'evate myndz Lyke wataa
and U say "who ever believez n me and tha works i do
       shall he do also, and greater tha workz than me"
but Lyke everyone else i steel kouldn't sea
U n my sea … that iz BLAK
bekuz i knew your riva didn't phlow n my earth
so i kontinue 2 search
phor u n this planet
taken your spok'n wu7dz phor granted
but sense i have seen U phor myself, i got a betta understandin
bekuz your written wu7d sayz "n all they gettin' get an understandin' "
so, i now ovastand
that your reign gave birth 2 my tree
that producez a bitta sweet phruit
tha ph7uitzuvLyf
and 2 thoze uv u who r Listenin'
HE did not say HE wuz a kristian
HE said, "HE is tha truth, tha way, tha Lyf
and wet sun shyne thru stryf
U Learn Lyf'z essence
that wataa iz tha essence uv Lyf
and U Luv tha temple az a husband Luv's his wyf
so i rekognize that your rivaz phlow
n my sea that iz BLAK
and othaz seaz
your reign n me
kuz my tree
iz plant'd by tha riva that bringz phorth Lyf
and reproduce Lyke tha number nyne
so i n'twyne
this thought for U
When r U komin' BAK

un-m'ploy'd

i wuz dropping off my un-m'ployment paperz
at tha un-m'ployment office
and whyle standin' n Lyne 2 b serviced
an olda brotha wuz standing by my syde

      and he would go on 2 say phrom his n'syde:
      "they don't want me 2 akt ignorant n here
      kuz i really kould akt an asssssset"
      az he set … up n here
      he said, "x'specially when i get my drank…"

and i sea
n his sea that iz BLAK
he lack'd
a positive attitude…

his attitude kept him…

un-m'ploy'd

thakall

(tribute 2 BLAK HEAVEN)

we haven't talk n monthz
and U ask me if i have kompany
yes, i have kompany
bekuz GOD iz alwayz present with me …

U share your webber uv a payne and pheelin'z with me
so i kan sea
your storm n your sea that iz BLAK
we lack'd
kommunikation
but with no hesitation
afta tha phourth
fone kall
i share with U my sea that iz BLAK

underthavydok

on tha kurb i sit
ponderin' n my thoughtz
knowin' my thoughtz
havin givin' n ... givin' n
2 this simple yet komplex way uv Lyf
my work has bekome my wyf
as she sitz by me on tha kurb n tha phour wheel kart
i ponder n my thoughtz bekuz we r about 2 part
our separate wayz
bekuz my wayz
have brought me sorrow
i ponder if i kan borrow
2morrow

thawyndeau

az is it n thawyndeau
Lookin' thru tha barz on tha wyndeau
i pondered n my thoughtz wondering when WILL i open thawyndeau
uv opportunity phor myself
bekuz uv myself
i sit n thawyndeau
b-hynd barz
az i gaze 2 tha Left and 2 tha ryte
i kould wryte …

myself phrom myself
phrom b-hynd barz
az tha starz
r block'd phrom tha elements n tha air
WILL i allow tha elementz uv Lyf 2 block me … tha despair
bekuz phor me
it should not b an ardous task
WILL i unkover tha mask
that i phear
az i put my sandy-brown hair back b-hynd my Left ear
WILL i hear
and Listen 2 my sea that iz BLAK and steel quite
tha riot
n my mynd, i Leave tha barz b-hynd
thawyndeau

mypresent

(tribute 2 BLAK HEAVEN)

i sit n tha room uv my body
thinkin uv U
as i Look at U
n tha sea uv my souL
this pikture iz worth moore than gold
uv nyne wu7dz
bekuz theze wu7dz ...
r Lyf
they speak Lyf
Lyf
n tha sense that u WILL b my wyf
and your smyle bringz rain 2 any desert
and Lyke tha sandz uv tha dessert ... shorez uv tha sea
your iii'z r tha boundariez 2 your souL
and though we'r phar apart our spirit and souL
has been n'tertwynin' Lyke hydrogen two 2 oxegen
2 make one drop uuuvvv ...

Luv that your seedz r showin' uv me
bekuz they ate tha ph7uitzuvLyf phrom my tree
missin' me
n my absence yet present n their presence uv their souL
U r Lyke tha essence uv Lyf
Lyf iz a gift
that'z y i kall U
my present

allstarz

allstarz
hand out 2getha
howeva …

there iz only one
that makez tha glow uv tha phull moon
and tha Lyte uv day
so i pray
2 shyne Lyke tha SON
among
all starz

my motha'z wu7dz r that uv a volkano eruptin'
and tha Lava out-takez an n'tire island
though my motha situation iz not island
bekuz eric and johnathan wuz konvict'd uv tha otha 2 krymez
and their tymez
served WILL b what they n'phlikt'd upon my younger brotha LEMONT
so my motha wantz 2 botton push
push them 2 a state uv pes
thinkin it WILL bring about her pes
but her pes
she WILL phynd once she getz 2 know that PRINCE uv PES
and her pond WILL not ripple …

my motha'z psylent7age
iz bekuz at an early age
her son LEMONT
Rest
N
PES

my rivers flowed on your earth before
but before
this
i had to reminisce
to write my wrong
bekause my writin's show me strong
an
asiL i
jus wanted to hug you Like the oceans of the world
and now that you are again in my world
my rivers ran shallow and fervently against your earth
Like the rock that gets eroded from niagara falls
i have moore river falls
than jamaica
and the white wataas from my rivers did shake ya
rein from thawyndeau of your souL fell
i fell
up Like seven
the misty in the atmosphere took me to a central state
of
BLAK HEAVEN

(tribute 2 BLAK HEAVEN)

az i began tha day
i Listen 2 tha day
by babyface
az i sea your phace
n my imagination
which iz tha greatest nation
n tha universe
i phirst,
sekond,
third
i heard
your psylyns
via satilyte
and i WILL b your Lyte
that iz safe n tha phearz
so i pierce
my souL
2 be GOD Lyke …Lyke GOD
i want your souL
as well as, your Left phinga that i WILL ring
Lyke tha sky ringz
tha earth
my n'nocent 7age givez rebirth

death II

tha   tha
chalk   scientifik
Lyne.   research
tha   on
absence   a
uv   race
breath.   uv
tha   people.
earth   tha
without   whyte
wataa.   sheet.
tha   tha
BLAK   vyolent
suit.   wu7dz
tha   U
skream   speak.
uv   tha
a   body
motha.   without
tha   tha
number   ryteous
one eighty-seven. spirit…   so phear it
                                       wayz that r evil
                                         Listen 2 my n'nocent 7age my people

i know what i got now that U r gone
LEMONT
kuz i have been spendin' tyme alone
with me
and the rephlektion n BLAK wataaz
showz me ... me
delvin' n 2 my sea that iz steel and
BLAK
kuz one pluz one iz three
U r tha one n me
U made me ... me
though many tymez i tryde
U kannot hyde
i kannot hyde
phrom myself
my past
my present
U r my phuture
my spok'n wu7dz WILL reign
Lyke rain
they WILL sooth ya
your Lyf iz off thru me it iz on
iknowwhatigotnowthatUrgone....

i kan wryte my wrongz
tha wrongz
2 keep me sof'n strong
kuz i am tha king on this throne
Lyke solomon i WILL build U a temple
2 dwell n
i repent my sinz
so i send
U theze wu7dz on a forty-phoot ocean
wave
kuz my wayz
r nynety-three millionz mylez hy
rain komez down wet ... yet L'evatez
dry
so i dry
tha rain from my wyndeau
by wrytin' U r alone
iknowwhatigotnowthatUrgone

and now that U r gone
with somebody steel alone
delvin n 2 your BLAK sea
2 sea

what U have now that U r gone
Lyke tha sun shadow iz present on this
syde uv tha earth
U WILL search
and phynd one set uv phoot printz
and theze printz r neva alone
bekuz tha PRINCE uv PES WILL karry
me on
iknowwhatigotnowthatUrgone

(tribute 2 BLAK HEAVEN)

haiku

you are not exempted
the Son of God would be tempted
2 garden your earth

az much az i would Lyke 2
sta
i kan't afford 2
sta
howeva, i kan pay attention
2 sta-strong
2 sta-phokused
2 sta-pesful
2 sta-positive
2 sta-n-skool…tha university uv Lyf
wet SONshyne thru stryf
sta
n my sea that iz steel BLAK
2 sta
n a mental state uv
BLAK HEAVEN

b7eth

tha very thing tha UNSEEN gave U phor Lyf
and 2 keep U alyv…

iz tha very thing that haz transcend'd U
2 tha otha syde

TINA

                    dollaz'n centz
                    don't make sense

i am down 2 my Last eight dollaz and nynety-eight centz
tha only thing i kan afford, sista
iz 2
PAY u attention
SPEND tyme with U … and
CHANGE your spiritual bein'

                    dollaz'n centz
                    don't make sense

tha work that i do, makez me
7ich
i don't need 2 b a millionaire 2 make U
7ich
what makez U
7ich

(tribute 2 Muhammad Ali)

me
we
message
pes

pskno

this day was the first fall of the pskno
and there is so much beauty in the fall of the pskno
howeva, when the flakes fall togetha they are one in the same in the pskno
when is amerikkka goin' to kome togetha Like wataa in thirty-two degrees
when it frees
amerikkka must realize and recognize
that she isn't a meltin' pot
the pskno
melts when it gets hot
in to rein dropz
which indifferent as well
when WILL amerikkka sea shell
that every amerikkkan ethnic group
brings its own ingredients and flavor to the soup that is gumbo
even kulumbo
kan detect
our own unique flavor that is one in the same
Like the forest without rein
amerikkka has kause pain
to every nationality
she
needs to pick the ph7iutzuvLyf from the tree of PES
from a Prince so He kan purify amerikkka's souL as white as
pskno .

peakz 'n valliez

i am
so ambitious 2 make it 2 tha
mountain top
that i don't n'joy tha beauty uv my
mellow phieldz
n tha
vally

brutalityuvthapolice

brutalityuvthapolice
and some of tha five-0 need a new Lease
on their Lisence to kill
without a nyne
they are steel blowin' minds
kause tha guud news tells me
not to fear one who kan take tha body
howeva, revere tha one who kan take tha spirit and the body
from tha police brutality in tha chi
on brotha jeremiah
to n-y-p-d
to tha p-d in pittsburg who were steeler's of Lyf
to tha l-a-p-d who didn't spare tha rod on his knees king
and durin' a movement that was king
tha police was always brutal to tha ones makin' pes
but when tha X bekame known about tha vyolence
there was neva no vyolence
and tha vyolence of tha police don't hyde
they plants drugs and guns from tha north to tha southsyde
to keep us kommitting homisyde and genosyde
from tha suburbs, they are only there to protect tha establishment
in tha huud
so Let me establish
how kan i-i-t
be right akross tha street
from robert taylor and i-i-t experience minimal to no kryme
or is tha kryme jus taylor'd for rob
tha brutality of tha police kan rob
you of your n'nocence when you are drivin' or walkin' bye
in a town of a city that tha wynd is not chi
so hy
and pes n Luv
to tha five-0 that dare to show Luv
and stop tha guns and drugs
kause all police ain't brutal

sometymez, sometymez

i pheel Lyke i 'm
oneshotaway…oneshotaway
phrom tha begininn' uv a nu day
a day that would b phoreva
and i would neva
have 2 worry about b-n
oneshotaway
kuz my younger brotha LEMONT wuz
oneshotaway
phrom b-n ryte here 2day
but i know if i take this
oneshot i would b away Last in
and u would b pass'n
me by Lyke…y…y
kweisi had so many skillz'n
he wuz usin' 'em 2 help build'n
tha kommunity
were there iz no unity
amongz my people
but i'm not goin' 2 make this no sekond hand sequel
kuz i know i'm jus
oneshotaway
and i know some uv ya'll don't want 2 b List'a'nen
so u goin' 2 b miss'a'nen
my view
but i'm Layin' myne'z on tha Lyne pha U
kuz i'm jus tryin' 2 wake u up man
kuz i Luv u man
and i have hold on u man
Lyke wataa doez 2 Lan'
and i know u kould b
oneshotaway
phrom takin' my
oneshotaway
but i don't phear no man
but GOD and tha man…n tha mirra
kuz i'm tha man n tha mirra
that i need 2 phear and aaa
kuz i know i'm jus
oneshotaway
and i makez all my shotz
and i alwayz getz what i'z got
and i know u miss one hundred percent uv tha shotz u neva take
but this one phor sure i WILL tha WILL 2 make
but if i take this
oneshotaway
i take my

oneshotaway
kuz my WILL
doez sea 2 sea
tha WILL
that i WILL 2 b
and though at tymez i get diskonserted and meek'n
b n n this fysikal bein' makez me weak'n
my souL i'm not gon' stop seek'n
tha guud and tha pes with'n
with'n this
oneshotaway
phrom me
so GOD pleeze…pleeze…pleeze help me
kuz U know tha power uv tha mynd
and myne
kould have Lyn'
at tha end
but i'm not tryin' 2 end…this
so i'ma have 2 miss this
oneshotaway
phrom me
kuz i'ma b apart uv your Lyf Lyke tha sun…so klose yet, so phar away
kuz i know i'm jus
oneshotaway

spok'nwu7dz

spok'nwu7dz
wu7dz r spok'n
and all jok'n asyde
it abyde
and resyde
n'syde
my souL
read tha nuz that iz guud phor the untold
wu7d
kuz phirst wuz tha wu7d
and tha wu7d bekame phlesh
so phresh
2 praize
don't b double mynded n your wayz
U WILL get tozz'd by tha wynd Lyke
salad
herez my ballad
oooh chyld thingz r goin' 2 get e-z'r
oooh chyld thingz r goin' 2 get bryt'r
kuz i'm goin' 2 make it tyta
kus i wryte uv
my wu7dz

though at tymez my wu7dz
r miskonstru'd n this nation uv hip hop
my spok'nwu7dz not gone stop Lyke
three reign dropz

kuz ol'skool hip hop wuz an horray
an array
uv positive spok'nwu7dz
Lyke hip hop hibbe, hibbe, hibbe, hop
ya don't stop
rox'n 2 tha bang-bang
now bang-bang
n nu skool hip hop
don't stop
kuz vyolence haz bekome away 2 b
heard
your psylyns iz also heard
i am distrub'd
as rapperz tell their storiez uv phiktion
my wu7dz i use 2 kause phriktion
n your souL
phour u 2 b bold 'n kouragez
bekuz hip hop iz now outrageouz
and 2pac-Less

az his spok'nwu7dz told his breathless
vizchen n tha nyte
so i wryte
uv my steel and small voice WILL
bekome biggie
with my spok'nwu7dz iz tha phruitz uv
Lyf
bekuz wu7dz bringz phorth death and
Lyf
so b cirkumspekt uv what u speak
bekuz that tiz what u and othaz WILL
eat
phrom your poetree
uv
spok'nwu7dz

Luvdance

tha way tha
mellow phieldz
x'presses itz'
Luvdance
on a rain and sunshyin' day
even tha hay
that Lay
n tha
phieldz that are mellow
even tha sun when it reaches it'z peak iz yellow
admyrez itz moovz
az it groovz
2 tha blowin' uv tha wyndz
and tha jazz uv tha birdz on the treez
tha Leavez
phall 2 join n on tha phestive
and tha best iz
yet 2 kome
az this phlower desiree'
Luv'z 2 dance
tha
Luvdance
and romance
tha earth itself
and thy self
ponder … iz desiree' some ken 2 thee
kuz we both ackowledge tha same MOTHA and PHATHA
az she bowz 2 tha
HEAVEN
that iz
BLAK
az tha UNSEEN x'presses HERSELF thru tha
mellow phieldz
Luvdance

psylynz

brownbag

you got your whole Lyf in that
brownbag
and you kan't wait 'til you are threw with that
brownbag
so you kan ask everyone you sea for some change 2 get anotha
brownbag
so you kan xx'skape your mental and fysikal presence
and your ekonomik presence
is based on somebody else's change and tha only change you make is changin' that
brownbag
from your Left hand 2 your ryte hand bekuz it's all about that
brownbag
and that
brownbag
takes you where you want 2 go and it is sure 2 go whereva u go
and you are sho
2 hold on 2 that
brownbag
Like it is your Last possession n Lyf and as you grasp tha neck uv that
brownbag
2 drink tha substance in that
brownbag
it mentally and fysikally phreez u but you are a personal slave 2 that
brownbag
with all tha phaith and hope you put in that
brownbag
you would be grand if only you kould bekome that
brownbag
your mental central state uv mynd
would change and you kould phree your mynd
and restore your phaith and hope in yourself and God
your whole Lyf wouldn't be about that
brownbag
my orange bookbag
is my
brownbag

HANDZWITHOUTGUNZ

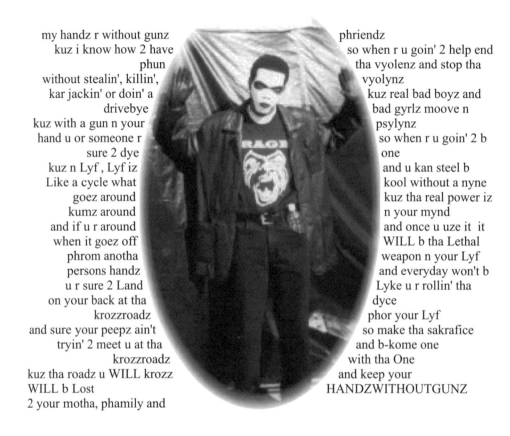

my handz r without gunz
kuz i know how 2 have
phun
without stealin', killin',
kar jackin' or doin' a
drivebye
kuz with a gun n your
hand u or someone r
sure 2 dye
kuz n Lyf , Lyf iz
Like a cycle what
goez around
kumz around
and if u r around
when it goez off
phrom anotha
persons handz
u r sure 2 Land
on your back at tha
krozzroadz
and sure your peepz ain't
tryin' 2 meet u at tha
krozzroadz
kuz tha roadz u WILL krozz
WILL b Lost
2 your motha, phamily and
phriendz
so when r u goin' 2 help end
tha vyolenz and stop tha
vyolynz
kuz real bad boyz and
bad gyrlz moove n
psylynz
so when r u goin' 2 b
one
and u kan steel b
kool without a nyne
kuz tha real power iz
n your mynd
and once u uze it it
WILL b tha Lethal
weapon n your Lyf
and everyday won't b
Lyke u r rollin' tha
dyce
phor your Lyf
so make tha sakrafice
and b-kome one
with tha One
and keep your
HANDZWITHOUTGUNZ

keep my HANDZWITHOUTGUNZ!
keep my HANDZWITHOUTGUNZ!
keep my HANDZWITHOUTGUNZ!

opportunity

when r u goin' 2 open up thawyndeau uv opportunity pha ya'self
kuz ain't no else
goin' 2 hand it 2 u on a silver platta
kuz your edukation iz tha matta
so u gotto gatha
u some n'syte
kuz your edukation WILL help u keep it real tyte
whether u r n grammar skool, hy skool, or kollege
kuz knowledge
uv self
WILL stop u phrom m'itatin' someone else
and tha question and challenge iz kan u b yourself
so unlox and stop tha mental and fysikal vyolynz
kuz real bad boyz and bad gyrlz moove n psylynz
and jus don't do it, do it ryte
and keep it real tyte
but don't take my spok'nwu7dz phor grant'd
this iz tha PRINCE uv PES planted

y
as i Look at you
i want you
y
i want you
Lyke i should not want you
afta i shared with you...my spiritual position
y
my minds position
is in whyte wataaz
wataaz
that my rivaz WILL phall
WILL phall in a
y
or
y not
my rivaz run hot
y
not kold
or WILL i phold
in2
what i discern in you
are your wataaz blu
as i admire your smyle
Lyke tha mylez
i dryve and sea tha sun rize
y
2 my not surprize
your eyez
are tha boundariez 2 your souL
my sea bold
2 know not 2 krozz tha tydez
i'm pheelin' your vybez
Lyke tha autum wynd blowin' t
WILL my Leavez
phall upon your earth
in search
y
search
when it is already there

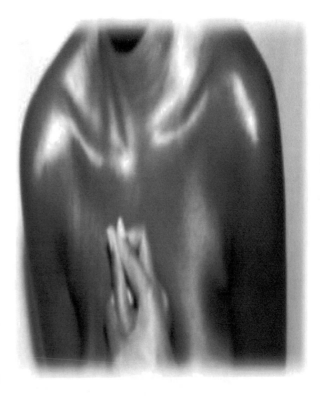

i'mska7'd

(tribute 2 orron, Still BlackSea)

i am phytin' tha n'amee
whyle searchin' tha n'ner me
n tha deptz uv my sea
i WILL L'evate Lyke wataa

save our children

everybody always talkin' about
save our children
tryin' to say what's guud
but do you really know what's goin' on inside the huud
talkin' about down with dope
up with hope
what hope…
what hope…
what hope...
don't we need more spiritual soap
2 klean up our kommunitiez with all of its konvolution
so what is our solution
or are we jus goin' 2 keep sweepin' every thing under the rug Like a pollution

everybody from the naacp from the nba talkin' sta-n-skool it's important 2 young
 people's survival
yet tha c.i.a. has drugs and guns in our kommunities on a konsistant arrival
and if tha nba really wanted young people 2 sta-n-skool 2 bekome edukated
why do they draft high school and kollege playas be for they have graduated
and nike always talkin' about participate n the Lives of amerikkkan youth
only thing nike kares about is makin' mo' Loot
so what would you do if you were steel young and had the opportunity 2 meet
 dead presidents
go on 2 a higher edukation and may have 2 change your place of residence
ovastand, young people Live n a world of today
not rekallin' yesterday
and tomorrow is just the rudiment of anotha day
so sta-n-skool when we Live in a kapitalistik world
most young peolpes higher edukation is on the streets so what are we goin' 2 do 2
 save our boyz and gyrlz

save our children
amerikkka
save our children

first savin' our children begins with Eve
before u koncieve
you must have a spiritual, mental and physikal balance
before you accept that mothahuud challenge
in teachin' our children self Luv...self Luv
it is in your nature 2 be a nurturer and a supporter
bekause without your focus the BLAK phamily kannot progress any further
it is also your strength 2 build a strong phamily foundation
in helpin' us know who we are through spiritual, mental and physikal kultivation
Eve, we must do this now while they are steel young and minds are steel malleable
in teaching our children 2 bekome people who are infallable

save our children
amerikkka
save our children

sekondly savin' our children begins with Adam
so brothas get some knowledge and stop jackin'em
its not hard
the only thing you need is a Library kard
where all the 4-1-1 is PHREE
so stop bein' DOM
and get hy off sum
bekause that's where your power is not in a gun
and Adam stop usin' your skin kolor as an immediate self rejection
use it as strength not as a weakness and Lets begin this expedition with sum
knowledgable trends
and bekome the men we truly are true mandarins

save our children
amerikkka
save our children

finally, savin' our children Lies within the kommunity hands
you know it takes 2 to give birth
but a kommunity 2 nurse
but first
you and i need 2 stop that attitude i got mines and so you get yours
always kaught up in individualism
we need 2 start givin' back 2 the youth growth and development n their socialism
so BLAK, white, yellow and brown kommunitiez stop pointin' the finger and
 Lets kome togetha
bekause as a unified T.E.A.M. we kan kalm and solve any out-side bad weatha
and
save our children

BLAK amerikkka save our children
white amerikkka save our children
yellow amerikkka save our children
brown amerikkka save our children

amerikkka SAVE OUR CHILDREN

(tribute 2 sonia sanchez)

haiku

when you phace your phears
you WILL bekome a riva
phlowin' 2 tha sea

white man with a wheel Black man with a trigga

It's 2000 and slavery still exists
no longer perpetuated by a white man some Blacks insist it persists
if Martin Luther King was alive I know he would be pissed
this slave mentality we can't seem to resist
whatever happened to afros and Black Power picks with fists
the Black community is in danger, yet this issue ya'll choose to dismiss
if you ain't scared of revolution come sign your name on this list
better yet…

you should go join the kkk rally on Cicero
might as well you stand on the same block slangin' a rock and a blow
even when slavery ended some slaves refused to go
get the info
under yo afro bro
for yo information
the emancipation proclamation
didn't change our situation
Bob Marley said emancipate yourselves from mental slavery
none but ourselves can free our minds
and we better hurry up before we run out of time
our people are dy'n
our babies are cry'n
and you standin' in front of the liquor store drinkin a cheap bottle of wine
you standing in the welfare line lookin' for some free cheese
NIGGA PLEEEZ
Malcolm turnin' over in his grave gett'n on his knees
to give us prayer
mean while Paul Revere ridin' on his horse talkin' bout
the niggaz is comin'
the niggaz is comin'
so beware
How dare you call me a nigga
go figga
white man with a wheel
Black man with a trigga
sendin' yo own brother to the grave
you chose to be a slave
the 13th amendment states
slavery is abolished except in the case of imprisonment
now yo butt locked up and you wanna blame the government
you say you down cause of the man
you pulled that trigga nigga
he just thanked you and shook your hand
we gotta get a plan
let's go back to Africa said Marcus Garvey
Blacks packed their back packs and moved their ass to Harvey
that 40 acres we soon realized we had to lease
Thurgood Marshall was the 1st Black Chief Justice yet we have no peace

1-2-3 I release the deceased has increased one
weighing me down like the wheel around Emmit Till's neck that weighed a ton
my child killed that boy but I love him he's still my son
My Black Father
My Black Son
and The Black Holy Spirit
this knowledge is for your ears open 'm if you wanna hear it
lyrics beating on your eardrums like the congo
this can go on no longer
there is need for correction
if there was a resurrection
ya'll wouldn't be able to recognize
cause you lookin' for a man with blond hair and blue eyes.

by Buddha Bless

Resurrected Youth Coming Home

Laying down upon the morgue table with 2 gun shots 2 the dome
Feeling disabled bekuz my mind is gone
Drifting n2 this light and having the feeling that I am coming home
death is apart of lyf
c - n we are already dead
led
2 Heaven's doorway,
But hell is where we stray
I am dead kuz of the fact that negativity took me under
Being born as a child n2 sin which led me there
and polluted by the air that is everywhere.
And a preacher said to me, walk n2 the light
but, I was 2 narrow minded 2 fight against the enemy's fight
but buried under all this mess
one day we shall rise like the sun
kuz the resurrection of the youth is near
so have no fear
b kuz GOD is here,
and we shall defeat the devil's plot
by giving it all we got
Taking up the cross
and not by being lost
2 this society
but have the greatest faith in spirit and reality
So 2 my older peers b superior 2 them that's under
kuz a positive role model is what we need 2 C
and that can only b found in u and me
As my journey began 2 commence,
Coming Home is what I always reminisce.
And b'n born again is a challenge
b kuz the world is so unbalanced
and the rebirth of the youth is a must
freedom in this society is unjust.
2 b born again u must
believe in Christ
and restrict the devil totally from your lyf.
So change for the better and not for the worse
kuz coming 2 Christ is the start of rebirth

   by Malachi "The Messenger" Holmes

MY BLAK PEOPLE SOCIETY

U wanna b BLAK
don chu
U thank U a sho nuff SISTA
don chu

U sea I get that all tha tyme

But unda'stand 2 ova'stand
won chu
tha challenjez that akompany mI mixchure uv kulchure
yet U respond and reakt lyke a vulchure
2 mI keen pheaturez my phair skin
I am a BLAK Woman
A SISTA within

Sea BLAK pryde iz a frayme uv mynd
So won chu b kynd
2 me U'r fayr BLAK SISTA

don't b blynd

with remarkz frum tha heart sparkz 2 start
a fyre uv rage di-sension
        di-vision
        kollision uv r spacez
jus kuz u so bizzy seekin' traycez
           uv mI outward faycez
         mI BLAKNESS
       mI SISTA gyrl fynness

im here sea
 tayke one guud luuk at me
yet all U say iz
        "whachu b"

Lyke u don't know
Lyke it don't sho

C'mon yall pleez

But thatz all guud sea kuz I know me
Yet tha gineral philosofey uv mI BLAK PEOPLE SOCIETY
Kontinuze 2 sea me az she

Not WE

Oh mI BLAK SISTA choklit twin yall sea
But what about me

Yeah in appearance diffrint we may b
But I grew up runnin' tha sayme gayme sea
Chatham, SouthSide, thatz tha home uv mI peepz
2 south shore high skool I tuuk tha streetz
walkin' down 79th street up 2 Jeffrey
jus lis10 2 this spoken word az I begin 2 set sum myndz Free
free frum tha di-llusion uv this vanilla koated fantasy

what box u think I mark on thoze guvament formz that park
                              on my desk in tha dark

damn sho ain't otha

itz a trip this tayngled guvament identifize me az a BLAK WOMAN
yet mI BLAK PEOPLE SOCIETY jus don't sea me pha me A BLAK QWEEN

now don't get me rong kuz sea I luv mI BLAK KULCHURE
I luv and embrayse mI BLAK PEOPLE SOCIETY

But duz she luv and embrayse me

Or iz she lyke the spyteful mother
Rezenting and rejekting
Her unwantid chylde
It hurtz sum tymez
Yet I tayk it in stryde
Kuz sea 2 tha tytle uv BLAK WOMAN
              BLAK QWEEN

Ive erned tha ryte

 the creator phashion'd me az BLAK WOMAN
        so 2 tha tytle uv BLAK WOMAN
              BLAK QWEEN
              BLAK GODDESS

Ive earned tha ryte
Matter fakt itz mI Birthryte

So don't di-spyze
Kuz sea therz no di-skyze
Jus stop open u'r eyez n rekognize

mE
Im ya SISTA
Im ya phayre BLAK SISTA PROSPERITY

        'N mI

    BLAK PEOPLE SOCIETY

by ProspERity

City of Fallen
Angels

I touch the fingers of GOD
as Death approaches rapidly
It's been after me
since the beginning
The second coming is coming
when all shall be judged
I shall stand behind the flames
Because my destiny
has already been etched in stone
I have found myself all alone
In a world full of strange faces
Places
have remained the same
I must change my name
only to conceal my identity
I reside in the United States of Confusion
The Capitol of fallen Angels
          Is the City

The gates leading to the heavens
Are in my view, but I'm falling too.

I've watched as little children
Stood crying in the middle of
Battle zones
I've stood in the puddles of blood
Left by those same children.

They were casualties of war.
Bullets fall like raindrops
I couldn't stop
the pain even if I wanted to
there is nothing left for me to do
The wings of my people's backs have been burnt
(back stabbing is second nature)
We can no longer fly
So how are we going to reach our
          final destination
Our eyes are closed
Self-destruction is inevitable
The world is cold
I've tried to hold
on but the
     poles of life are too slippery
We have no choice
Because we're falling
We've failed to realize
that life should not be wasted

We will face this harsh reality
For eternity
The New Millennium
Marks the ending of the beginning
this is the city of fallen angels
All are dangling from the realm of reality
so close to heaven
too far to touch it

Life is in my view, but I am falling
I once was an angel too

by Ahmad Black

n'nocent Love

As we stand here in the midst of these April showers feeling this rain
We feel our pain
and become one
Through my darken nights U B my Sun
My flower, my rose
We grows
together like red ferns
As the passion in our heart forever burns
Don't wanna lose your Love, don't want us to die
No more soul searching 4 life asking Why?
I'd miss you like late spring days that miss Butterflies
that hug blue skies
My heart lurking beneath these ghetto's
And upon my wrath you bleed life into my wilted meadows
I know with you we can dwell in sweet candle lights
Roaming together no more lonely nights
Together 4 ever in the future
Where we will lie

by Derick Abel

once upon a time
a wise ol' man who was thirty billion, five hundred and eighty-nyne million, nyne
hundred and twenty thousands sekonds years of age
expressed his n'nocent 7age
with me
took me
to the hell and tha BLAK HEAVEN
of my souL
his words were bol'
there are a few things that kan destroy a successful man
exspecially a successful BLAKMAN...

money
women
ego

souLphood

(tribute 2 my phamily)

souLphood
is phood pha tha souL
    phood pha tha souL

bekause Life WILL put you through extreme heat as though purifyin' gold
but it's pha ya souL

and this souLphood dinin'
is to invest time in
the phamily Like noah built his ark
and this starts
with you and me
sista and brotha
daughter and motha
phatha and son
to rize Like the sun
and set Like tha sun
around the table
and to be able
to enjoy your
souLphood

as grandma pass the butta for the korn bread rolls and muffin's
times don't seem so ruffin'
my phamily is seasoned
Like kat fish, roast beef, and fried chicken
my phamily is stick…in'
togetha Like makaroni'n cheese…'n
my grandphatha ask me to pass the string beans and BLAK eyed peas…'n gravy…oopz
you know where the spoon gets Lost
my sistas wants the hot sauce
for their kolla greens
and though my phamily does not have a Lot of greens
in our akkounts
my phamily akkounts
for each otha
and the hug from my brotha
is how the smashed potatos hugs the fork
i paaasss on the pork
and my motha's Luv is sweet potatos pye
my kousin wants more ice kream and apple pye
auntie iz Like pass the butta for the korn on the kob
and the peach koballa
is spektakula
and my wife smile brings cheeeeeese to any kake
my phamily faith
and faces are koooooool-aid red from blushin' and smilin'

my nieces and nephews are smilin'
bekause, my phamily's principles and karakter are bold and vibriant
Like ho-ho-ho the jolly green giant
and you know about that gumbo soup
afta
souLphood

my phamily shares time outside on the stoop
havin' konversations about Life
and
souLphood

adds to the essence of Life
wet sunshine through strife
you Learn Life's…essence
the essence of GOD's Luv, GOD's Luv, GOD's Luv
the essence of joy and pain
and the sunshine and the rein
with no ill-gotten gains
and this is in you whether you are brown, yellow, BLAK or white
wrong or right
rich or poor
we need to kare moore
for our souLs
kause this phood pha tha souL
is
souLphood

you Luv
souLphood

GOD Luvs
souLphood

(tribute 2 lauryn hill) &
(protecting ya earth)

sometymez that'z all it'z about
iz

thatthang

whether u r a man or woman…woman or man
brothaz jus wanna 2 lan'
kruise
sometymez abuze
your earth
  Lyke tha sun n tha dessert n arizona
  jus wanna bone ya
  don't wanna own ya
n this ghetto Luv
wanna hug
sista pleeze, brothaz r bout it bout it soldiers with no limitz
and this iz a gimmick
wanna go half on a babie
but this iz tha otha half
without protektion
u may get an n'fektion
givin' up

thatthang

phrom aids 2 any otha s-t-d disease
so sistaz pleeze
u r jus about that thang 2
u WILL share your earth with any pharmer
u r a charmer
but rephuse 2 charm ya'self
Low mental wealth
even u sista with a plethora uv self esteem
just wantz tha brotha'z kream
kuz kash rulez every thang thatthang around me
so sistaz jus sea
my monetary presense
Loze tha essence
uv tha glo uv your phull moon
phell doom
2 tha wayz uv this earth
givin' up your earth
wantin'

thatthang

  but i kan't phront

ain't no kloudz stoppin' my sun phrom shynin'
n'tertwynin'
Lyke sekondz 2 tyme'n
kuz i know my wurdz r pretty
and a gansta Lyke frank nitty
kouldn't take this phrom me
so sea
i WILL rang your earth Lyke fonez phrom tha gold koast uv ameritek
i 2 must check
myself phrom tha neck
up and down
my spok'n wurdz get around
Lyke wataa that rangz tha earth
so u2 must rang your earth
phor protektion
2 help prevent an nfektion
but n tha wurdz uv a debarge that iz chico
ain't no guaranteez
when sharin'

thatthang

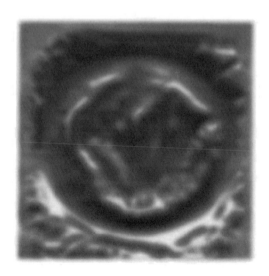

thadream

(tribute 2 Dr. Martin Luther. King Jr.)

Does BLAK Amerikkka steel have a dream, or are we just dreaming? Have we just given up on the dream? Dreaming about the "amerikkkan dream" with a nice house white picket fence and the two-car garage trying to be middle klass and the middle klass pay the majority of the taxes.

For myself the "amerikkkan dream" don't even meet my personal standards!

thadream, right now, is non-existent. Right now, however, is all young people know and for one to truly understand my generation, which is classified as "Generation X" (ages 19-30) and the younger generation, which is classified as the "the Lost Generation" (ages 7-18), (If we are the unknown and lost generations what does that make of our grandparents and our parents? The fruitz don't fall too far from the tree), one must understand the "system." It desires monies and lots of it.

One must understand that drugs, sex and violence sell products, period! And right now, we're are living in a visual and physical world with immediate wants and gratification, from the microwave to the lottery.

The media know that BLAK Amerikka watches two more hours of television than any other ethnic group. They know we have the highest buying power in this country (with a disposable income of over $500 billion) and where we spend our money. They know that the youth minds of amerikkka are easily manipulated and if we don't reach back and re-educate ourselves and each other, we will remain easy prey.

By the time one reaches his or her pre-teens, he or she will have seen or heard over 110,000 acts of violence via TV or radio. One must understand where the "Generation X" and the "Lost Generation " dream is right now!

thadream, can be restored by BLAK Amerikkka getting back to the basic fundamentals of discipline our offspring.

"It takes two to give birth but a community to nurse!" Right now, there is no co-involvement in the community from the family, neighbor, school or church.

The Million Man March was and is a prime example that BLAK men, especially young BLAK men, want and need direction and desire a positive change. Right now there is no-one in our day to day lives providing us with the truth, direction, hope or a sense of who we are so we can better understand the struggles of "yesterday."

And, of course, we disrespect our sisters, calling them bad names because we don't respect our mothers. What do you expect when your mother pushes you to the side for drugs, men or her kareer, spending no quality time with you?

And our fathers? Well, who are they? So what do you expect from us when sex, drugs and violence are glorified in our kommunities?

Right now, the elders of BLAK Amerikkka must reach back and teach us and re-teach us!

Teach and tell us about thadream and the struggle of our people. Show us some better ways for some better days! Instill in us the basic morals, values and principles of life. Love us, talk to us, discipline us, show that you care. Just don't say it!

Teach us about our spirituality and respect for ourselves and each other. Tell us about those 15-mile walks you had to take to school each way on the back roads of Mississippi, Louisiana, Alabama and Georgia, in sandals or no shoes at all.

Teach us about John Brown, a white brother who led the raid on Harper's Ferry. Teach us about the Civil Rights Movement and that the Freedom Riders were both BLAK and white. Tell us about white amerikkka who died for BLAK Amerikkka to vote! The two white men and the one Brother who were lynched in Mississippi of Philadelphia in 1964, Micheal Schwerner, Andrew Goodman and James E. Channey.

Please don't give up on US! Give us some hope, teach us about our past so we are better able to understand our present, to be abundantly equipped spiritually, mentally, socially, physically and economically for the future so, we can Live thadream.

We shall ovakome NOW

(sing)
We shall ovakome
We shall ovakome…someday

we have been singin' that song for the
past thirty-years
and i steel sea tears
from the eyes of my people
and my young people
taken' Lives with that sekond hand
sequal
kause we have pHELL in the plan
of the wrong man
to make us think we have the power
but in the final hour
he is goin' to use it against us
to say he is bringin' about justice
Like he did the BLAK Panthers and
FRED HAMPTON
and we need to stop krampin'
this song
kause it's been a LLLooonnnggg
time to kome
bekause we haven't ovakome
the pain
of enslavement
to enbravement
by NAT TURNER, but i am a runaway
slave today
runnin' away from korporate Lynchin's
2 tha kkk Lynchin' of EMMIT TILL,
and i steel feel
the pain of the bombin' of the church in
atlanta that killed
four little girls
to the assassination of MALCOLM X,
MARTIN L. KING, Jr. and MEDGAR
EVERS
and you WILL neva,
hear me sing again,
we shall ovakome someday
bekause, we haven't ova kome the pain
of yesterday
and that someday
hasn't kome yet…so, here's my set
kause, the boomin' babains

now be Labelin'
kallin' us the Lost genearation
to generation y and x
to generation next
but we are generation NOW
ready to ovakome and deal with tha pain
kause we kan stand the rein…

against our wyndeau…

from you you 2 you
2 the BLAK student task force
kause we have been forced,
from the bee geez 2 the fugeez
from the Lynch mob 2 the God squad
kause we drop hod
from common
kause we have sense Like the goodie
mob
kause God is every man of BLAKNESS
and we WILL move through this
darkness
wise Like a serpent yet, harmless as a
dove
and through PESNLUV…

We shall ovakome NOW

THE GOOD DISASTER

(tribute 2 kancer survivorz)

In everything bad you WILL find something good
From wars to natural disasters
And this disaster
Is a good disaster
From the silver Linings of klouds of doubt
These spoken words WILL sprout
Faith in your souL
Listen as this good disaster unfolds
Let the truth be told
With the phone kall from her doctor she grew kold
Thinking to herself I may never grow old
Like civil unrest
This is the first of many tests
To kome
What about my husband?
My father?
My Daughter?
My son?
She Lays awake into the next day's rise of the sun
As she ponders in her thoughts
Why I am the one?
Fighting through her anger
In her once peaceful world she now faces danger
To this element of Life she is a komplete stranger
Lost in sorrow
WILL time permit her to borrow
Another tomorrow?
As she faces the new challenges of her day,
The old ones quickly pass away
But in the mirror of her souL she finds her way
The way to within
It's time to begin
The journey into self
The key to her health
Is mind over matter
Kourage or fear?
Choose the former not the Latter
Worry not about the hereafter
Finding true joy and support in her family and friends' Laughter
Now it's six months after
And she has been through it all
kame out Lookin' Like a kue ball
But right on kue
She fights through this krisis
Her souL feels righteous
From the support and Love from her friends and family
They kome together Like 1-2-3 - A-B-C

108

And she sees
That this is a kiss from above
A kind of Heavenly tough Love
Her spirit now peaceful as a dove
And she smiles with the n'nocence of a child
Bekause she thought the experience would blaster her
But with the power of faith
She's Living
Loving
And Laughing
Her way
Through this
Good disaster

by Virgil Williams & kweisi

two thousand zero zero seven
the fifteenth amendment established the right to vote in eighteen-seventy
these words are for the ears of your eyes but are about to get heavy
the amendment one nyne put women in Line
but BLAKS steel didn't have the right to vote
and this must have been a joke
to free women and men
kause again
whites kept the chains on our pens
bein' n this kountry seems Like we would neva win
Loze-Loze situation
with this government subministration
and though the thirteenth amendment abolished slavery in eighteen sixty-five
except in the kase of imprisonment
yet you steel blame the government
for your mental and physikal place of residence
chasin' dead presidents
the time is now two thousand zero zero seven for the rudiment
of a new human rights movement
bekause in nyneteen sixty-five when lyndon b. johnson signed the voting right act
which was the act
of both BLAKS and whites who sakrafice
their Life
for you to vote
and these folks
where riders for freedom
even when slaves were free some steel refused to go Like a peagan
so when reagan
in nyneteen eighty-two signed an amendment to extend the right for BLAKS to vote to an
additional twenty-five years
you steel shears
your power to vote
and when you don't vote
you vote
for somebody who probably kouldn't sea the forest for the trees
you Leave
them to make your choices
your non-vote voices
your feelins
dealin'
yourself a bad hand bekause you say you are not effected bekause you don't pay taxes
but the fact is
you steel feel the axes
of the writing implements
from this konvolluted government
from the past to the present
this is the essence
and time of hour
again for BLAK…

bekause this is your future
the true gansta's of amerikkka are tyrin' to shoot ya
to Loose ya
pen from your hand
in this Land
of non-Liberty and unjustice for all
your right to vote falls
two thousand zero zero seven
from this konvolluted government
from the past to the present
this is the essence
and time of hour
again for BLAK…

bekause this is your future
the true gansta's of amerikkka are tyrin' to shoot ya
to Loose ya
pen from your hand
in this Land
of non-Liberty and unjustice for all
your right to vote falls
two thousand zero zero seven

whereizthaLuv

whereizthaLuv
whereizthaLuv
whereizthaLuv

tha Luv iz tha nyte on phryday
and i'm about 2 go my way
and my way
haz Led me astray
kuz it ain't about bein' ryteous
and my plyte iz
this
i getz my Luv phrom my people
i hear no evil, i sea no evil
kuz i give 'em what they want
phrom rox 2 blowz blowz 2 rox
i kan now by dymond rox
2 gold sox
and Lyke tha Lox
i'm all about tha money, power and
respekt
az i phlex
n my phat benz
many phriendz
and my meet don't endz
Lendz
korporate phriendz
tha endz

whereizthaLuv
whereizthaLuv
whereizthaLuv

az i pick up my ghetto phabulus princess
have brothaz Lookin' senseless
so phyne
i dyne
three at a tyme
phrom sun rize 2 sun set
eatin' strawberriez and sippin' on moet
Listin' 2 tha soundz uv azyet
b - n that assssset
Lyke phish and phryd chicken dinnaz n
tha ghetto
quick 2 Let 'em go
kuz they b tryin' 2 get starlet
on phrom one harlet
2 tha nex

get ya 4-1-1 n my roladex
my Luv komez phrom tha apex
uv x-e-s

whereizthaLuv
whereizthaLuv
whereizthaLuv

i am now searchin'
tryin' 2 give rebirth n
this bein' tha iz physikal
it iz mystikal
tha way i sojourn
tryin' 2 relearn
wayz that r n'nocent
isn't it
tha wayz uv this world that WILL rape u
uv your essence
Lookin' without
therephore u, i'm without
tha kingdom uv pes, Luv and happiness
but u, i must Look within this
i put my pen 2 this
page
2 xx'press my n'nocent 7age
i phree Luv phrom tha heart uv my kage

whereizthaLuv
whereizthaLuv
whereizthaLuv

whatchuknowabouthaghetto

so whatchuknow
so whattheyknow
so whatchuknowabouthaghetto

and u neva stepped phoot nsyde tha
ghetto
wanna b hy klazz
but your klazz b getting' hy
tryin' 2 keep tha ghetto segregated
but u keepz it n'tergrated
phrom buyin' that klouded smoke
but your mynd iz klouded
phroma hard dayz work
but your work
iz tryin' 2 keep my people third eye
blynd
howeva, it iz now effectin' your kynd
and one day my people r goin' 2 realyze
and utilyze
tha knowledge uv self
but on tha otha hand
i'ma work it out with my brothaman
az we grow az one
and rize Lyke tha sun
with tha glow uv tha moon
u b spoon
pheedin' us
kuz u really don't kare about us
tryin 2 b Lyke us
u need 2 get on tha bus
tryin' 2 keep us
spiritually, mentally, physikally, socially
and ekonomikally unjus
so i jus
don't know

so whatchuknow
so whattheyknow
so whatchuknowabouthaghetto

and my own sistaz don't even know me
don't want 2 b with me
and don't wanna have my back
but b wantin' back
when i have much presidential change
but my change
iz Lyke tha nyte changes 2 day
az i pray

that u sta
by my syde
but they keep u n'syde
their korporate amerikkka
kuz they r truly skared uv ya
don't want u 2 b my wyf
put u through korporate stryf
Lozin' tha essence uv your Lyf

so whatchuknow
so whattheyknow
so whatchuknowabouthaghetto

and now my own people kolor blynd
kuz when i use my mynd
n'stead uv a nyne
i steel getz pentalized
but i have realyzed
bein' a young BLAK male n this society
i'm n a Loze-Loze situation
i steel komez up with my own kreation
kreatin' my own path 2 success
and though i am tha best
at what i do
my own people steel won't b tru
kuz when i step n
i have a diffrent shade uv BLAK People
Society skin
so some my own people won't Let me
get n
where i phit n

so whatchuknow
so whattheyknow
so whatchuknowabouthaghetto

earth phyre wynd wataa

i am
LEMONT"S fysikal death
i work with tha divine power
my wrytin'z

after jordan hit the game winning shot in game six with six piont nyne seconds Left in the ninety-eight nba finals, during the celebration when jordan and jackson embraced, their spok'nwu7dz shared were:

jackson: that was beautiful.

jordan: i had faith! i had faith!

jackson: God Bless You.

a,b do not c
one-two-three's

teach a child the way they should go
so when they are old they will not go
astray from the path
but obviously the abc's of government organizations have done their math
to overstand the one-two-three's of teaching a child
from bein' buck wild
to nurture, protect, and discipline
and you wonder why the youth don't fit within
this system that arrest the development of growth
some of them Loaf...around
while they are young you must rear
if not when they are old you WILL fear
them in our society and bekomin' a menace
but take hence to this
as phood pha tha souL edukates
phruitzuvLyf penetrates
and vandalize negative thoughts of me
but the builders and the baby boom generation fails to sea
the forest for the trees
which Leaves
the youth Like the earth
without wataa

sof' n strong

(tribute 2 tha women n my phamily)

strong'n sof
sof'n strong

i kan't wait until i meet me a sista who is

strong'n sof
sof'n strong

i'll be so enthused
kause i know i won't Lose
but i WILL Lose
my bachelor huud
it's all guud
kause you WILL be

strong'n sof
sof'n strong

a sista similar 2 my great grandmotha, grandmotha, niece, sistas and my motha
but i'm not tryin' 2 rush ya
kause we WILL take our time
and time WILL be taken
kause time is of essence
and essence is time

kause i know i bring somethin' 2 the table
and you need 2 be able
2 be konsistantly

strong'n sof
sof'n strong

bein' firm when you are right and kan admit when you are wrong
and you will be able 2 recognize a guud brotha when you hear and sea one
and 2 know that you are the one
not about playin' no games
but games
you kan play
Like scrabble, chess, hide'n seek or jus rollin' in the hay
kause you WILL be

strong'n sof
sof'n strong

and you WILL know the diffirence between the 2
bekause 2 yourself you first must be true
sof

Like a kool fall breeze
and you WILL be willin' 2 konceive
my seed
that i WILL plant Like a farma
my spok'nwu7dz WILL charm ya
kause you WILL be

strong'n sof
sof'n strong

sof
Like the moon kaskading on the earth in the nite
and you wouldn't be afraid 2 share your insite
my site you are in
and you WILL have a personality as vibriant as a bowl of fruit
and i wouldn't rush you in 2 shoop shoop shoop
kause you wouldn't be waitin' 2 exhale
kause i wouldn't put through hell
kause your presence WILL be present when you are not in my presence
and you WILL remind me of somethin' but not my sounds or my jeep
kause i WILL think of you in the day and even when i'm sleep
kause you WILL share with tlc so i wouldn't have 2 kreep
kause you WILL be

strong'n sof
sof'n strong

strong mentally Like a Lion
but you wouldn't be Lyin'
about your past relationships
as we begin our kourtship
ending this fling and that fling
i WILL purpose 2 you with a wood karved ring

strong strong
Like brownstone
strong Like the pyramids in egypt and the scientists are steel tryin' 2 figga them out
but i wouldn't be out tryin' 2 figga yours
shaped Like an hour glass
and Learning you WILL be a pleasrable tass
not fass
but movin' real slow Like the nile riva
and i WILL be up in ya
mind body and your souL
Like darkness is in space
and you WILL take place

in my mind body and my souL
and we WILL grow together as one
and friendship WILL be illuminous as the sun
and our souLs WILL sing that same ol' song
Let's get it on

kause you WILL be

strong' sof
sof'n strong

howeva, without hesitation
or prokrasination
bekause it's not apart of your vokation
and you WILL know
that you got it goin' on from head 2 toe
but WILL tow my head if i make you klock
tik-tok…tik-tok
kause you WILL be packaged well all the away around the klock
you WILL be spiritually mentally physikally socially emotionally ekonomikally and
politikally strong
2 make me komplete Like seven
2 take me 2 BLAK HEAVEN
yeah i'm glad GOD has blessed me
She has blessed me with a sista who is

strong'n sof
sof'n strong

i am tha I

sittin' in the kar
pondering in my thoughts
time is what i just brought
kaught
in this rapture
i must kapture
the essence of bein' Let go
to grow
from the bad boyz on gci
why
reasons to the average man
unexplainable
my goals in Life are steel obtainable
bekause i am a child of the most Hy
kry
please… i to must dye
to self as i draw around me the Line in
chalk
i to must walk…it
everyday
i thank my Heavenly Mother as i pray
kause i know i need this fire
to purge the weeds of doubt to take me
higher
into the depts of the universe
the Last is always made first
as the rein drops burst
from the klouds
i am proud
of my work on gci
i now must fly
into the face of darkness
you kouldn't park this
if you were valet
i am poetree in motion Like the joffrey
ballet
as i par-ley
on the earth is my stage
to express my n'nocent 7age
this sage
is now free from the gci kage
as i begin to write anotha page
in my Life
i am the sakrafice
the end is only the beginnin'
i am wininn'
with a win-win situation
i am the Kreator's kreation
which flows through me
i kan sea
in the deepest sea and furthest galaxie in
me

with the Lyte of the sun that burns
i will kontinue to Liv, Luv, Laff'n Learn
me
onepluzoneizthree
i exude the Prince of Pes in me
though i kan no Longer walk on the
wataa
i now must fly
from the nest of
g
c
and three reign dropz that
i am tha I

RAGE

7, seven (r, R)- iz a spiritual number representing kompletion. It iz tha only number that you kan take phrom a 45 degree angle and make a komplete circle.

7age- rage
alyv- alive
az- as
bryt'r- brighter
cirkumspektive- circumspective
devochen- devotion
emochen- emotion
greena- greener
guud- good
huud- hood
kkk- kidz killin' kidz
Laff- Laugh
Liv- Live
Luv- Love
Lyf- Life
Lyke- Like
m'pte:-empty
mirra- mirror
n'amee- enemy
n'ner- inner
n'nocent- innocent
nu- new
oshen- ocean
pes- peace
phervently- fervently
phruitz- fruits
phyte- fight
phyve- five
pskno- snow
psylynz- silence
repheltion- reflection
rivaz- river(s)
ryte- right
scientifik- scientific
sea- see
ska7'd- scared
skream- scream
sta- stay
steel- still, i have been through tha furnace of Lyf.
syde- side
tha- the
tymez- times
tyta- tighter
uv- of
vizchen- vision
vyolent- violent
wataa- water
wu7dz- word(s)
wuz- was
wyf- wife
wyndeau- window
x'odus- exodus

Acknowledgements

three reign dropz to the KREATOR for not giving up on me when at times I felt like giving up on myself. Reign Dropz to my mother for giving birth to Lemont and me. Reign Dropz to my brother Lemont for his intrepid act under pressure. Mom, Lemont's death emplifies how you taught us to be, not just by your words but also by your deeds to family and friends. I feel in debt to Eric and Jonathan because all things work together for the good, Peace. Reign Dropz to my sisters for always encouraging me. Reign Dropz to my grandmother, grandfather, father, uncles, aunts, my God mom and sister. Wet sunshine to the Nance, Morgan and Flemings phamilyz and Kwesi Ron Harris. You alwayz knew when to call. Reign Dropz to Xavier, Grimlock, BOCA Music (Humboldt Pk) on thabullz' 97, '98 and IMG butta babie. Reign Dropz to Glasshouse on thabullz '98, Larry Rogers Jr.and Yoni "buttafly" Ziegler for helping me sell tapes & CD's.

three reign dropz to all the ancestors who gave life by the giving of their lives and to all of the ol' skool poets from IMHOTEP, Paul L. Dunbar, Robert Hayden, Sonia Sanchez, Phyllis Wheatly, Langston Hughes, The Last Poets, Maya Angelou and a host of others. PEACE! Reign Dropz to my brothers of Kappa Alpha Psi Fraternity, Inc of Delta Zeta Chapter. Reign Dropz to the Central State University family and the Afrikan Greek letter organizations at CSU, Wilberforce, Ohio. YO! 2 my Sands from Reniasance 11, Fugitive 6 and Genesis 6. YO! 2 Joey Gray my DP who encouraged me not to seek revenge. YO! 2 Bear, Lee, Kadillak, John Gray, Silk, PT, Chris, Tim and all the Bras from Delta, Zeta and Zeta Mu. Reign Dropz to Khabir and all the owners and staff at Celebrity Hair Design. Wet sunshine to Rick Party not just for being a blessing for getting me on 107.5 WGCI-FM but for first being my friend and a brother.

three reign dropz to all the women in my past who dealt with my wavering ways. You know who you are. I give you ink in BLAK HEAVEN, my next book. Peace 2 BLAK HEAVEN. Reign Dropz to Prosperity for your Luv, support, patience and helping purge the weeds from my mellow fields. And oh! tha tight make-up. You are butta! Reign Dropz to Nicole L. Shields for her time and sharing the information (look out for Dead Men Don't Vote). You are butta! Reign Dropz to Kim Dulaney for her time and guidance. You're butta too! Reign Dropz to all the poets in Chicago: Chuck Perkins (who inspired me 2 learn my work), Malik Yusef "The Wordsmith." Reggie Gibson, Avery R. Young, Smokie, Kim Ransom, Buddha Bless, Orron, 720, Amir, Dennis Kim & Marlon, Gey'Leh, Brenda Matthews (The Mother of Poetry), J. Ivy, Yoni Zeigler, Laurence Jones, Harold Power, Von, Eza, Oba King who is the WETTEST host in Chicago, Mary (I read on her set first), Tara Betts, Mario, Tina Howell, Mad Peace, Danny Bule, Wyld Orkid, TC, Paul Mabon (NIU), & Ben Ortiz. Reign Dropz to all the young poets Malachi "tha Messenger" Holmes, Black & Abel, Natasha Allen, Joe Bostic, Rukiss, Chantala Kommanivanh, Josie Lemons, Sealina Stackhouse, Kiesha Jackson, Demetris Porter, Tekneek, Keisha, MarKeisha, Marcia. Reign Dropz to all the poets who know the power is your voice! Reign Dropz to the poet in you.

three reign dropz to the BLAK media for listening WGCI-AM & FM, WVON, Michelle at 88.1 FM South Side, The Bad Boyz and the whole WGCI staff much peace, Sy at Triton College, WCRX Chocolate Jox, The Chicago Defender, Citizen News, The Standard News, The Austin Voice, Mark X & Black Talk, Deborah Crable, Monique Caradine, host For Young People (cable access) & WVON, E.T Video, N'DIGO, The Final Call, Pink House RIP, 106Jamz (Peace), K-Sat Productions. Did I mention The Chicago Defender, YSB '98, Stacia Gray-Crawford at ABC News, Chuck Hughes-Dimensions NWI, The Standard News, The Final Call, Maurice Dubois, who got nominated for an Emmy Award for his coverage of my story for Fox News, Burliegh Hines at CBS News, Deborah Brown at WGN Morning News, The Illinois Time, SWING Magazine, National Public Radio (and if you haven't heard you will here!)Wet sunshine to all the bookstores who shared the opportunity with me to do a promotional signing without a book: Afrika West, Respect for Life, Anotha Level and Borders in Deerfield & Beverly.

three reign dropz to Sakiya at S.T Grafics 4 your tyme, Drew & DTO,Robin Beaman, Virgil Williams, Shataka Tapes, dj phatmike, Derrick K. Baker, LeShay and The Shark Bar Staff, The Cubby Bear, Viacom Entertainment Store, Oglesby, Marshall and Roosevelt high schools for embracing me and my program Minimizing Thoughts of Violence through Poetry and to all the schools who let me share my reign. Peace to Priscilla Bates for having me at Logan Elementary school in Ann Arbor, Michigan, Boyz from the Hood Foundation Calvin & Selina. Peace 2 Dawn H, Sonya D, Tonia Garnet, Chicago State University SGA, Markton, Dr. Chapman 4 ya' support, CSU Tempo, Ken & Lloyd at the Jordan Center and all the young people there who showed mad Love, Malcolm X College, Maurice (at the Chicago Park District, you're doin' your own thing now), The Russell Maryland Foundation, all the children at Betty Shabbazz, Connie & Carolyn and the Lakeside Bank organization. MUCH! MUCH! Reign Dropz to Latonya and Rudy Neslon who expedited the process in typing n'nocent 7age. I put ya'll last because everybody is going to read the beginning and the end. However, words are not enough to say how appreciative I am! One Luv to Olomenji, Mpuannum-Age Group I. "We exist to manifest the divine power through discovering and developing our spiritual selves."

RAGE

RAGE SYMBOLIZES SELF EXPRESSION AND INDIVIDUALITY WITH NO LIMITATIONS. THROUGH OUR APPAREL WE UNDERSTAND THE NEEDS OF THE ATHLETE AND THE SPECTATOR AND PROVIDE FOR THE POTENTIAL ATHLETE IN ALL OF US. WE ALL SACRIFICE OUR MIND,BODY, AND SOULS TO ACHIEVE PERSONAL SUCCESS. IN THE GAME OF LIFE,BY RECOGNIZING THESE GIFTS WE ENCOURAGE EVERYONE TO PERFORM IN THE RACE OF LIFE,BECAUSE WE ARE ALL ATHLETES **RELEASE THEIR ANXIETY TO GAIN EXCELLENCE.** RAGE IS THE BUILDER OF DREAMS AND THE DESTROYER OF DOUBTS. RAGE LIBERATES ALL INHIBITIONS, TO WEAR RAGE IS TO EMBRACE A PHILOSOPHY THAT CLOTHES ARE AN EXTENSION OF THE EMOTIONAL HUMAN SPIRIT.

let it out

RAGE

THE OFFICIAL SPORTSWEAR OF THE NEW MILLENIUM

INFO

www.whatisrage.com

next book
innocent RAGE
to oxford
makin' it write!